The Sea Angler's
STEP-BY-STEP GUIDE TO
Bait and Rigs

emap

Acknowledgements
Editing: Mel Russ
Tackle: Meil Mackellow
Bait: Alan Yates
Photographs:
Terry Begg
Matthew Roberts
Tom Bailey
Artwork: Sea Angler Studio

ISBN 9780953308705

Produced by
Publishing Promotions **PP**
1 High Street
Princes Risborough
Bucks HP27 0AG

First published 1998 by
Emap Active Ltd
Bushfield House
Orton Centre
Peterborough PE2 5UW

Reprinted 2001, 2002, 2003, 2004, 2005 (twice), 2006, 2007

Welcome to the world of sea angling

This is the first book *Sea Angler* magazine has ever published... and it's packed from cover to cover with practical information to make you a better fisherman!
You can buy the best tackle in the world but if you aren't fishing with the right type of terminal rig or have the appropriate bait on the hook then your chances of catching are very much reduced. This book is designed to improve those catch rates and help you enjoy your fishing more. Study the rigs carefully, tie your own and then get out there and catch those fish.
You will note that in many instances we have used Dave Docwra Uni-Trace accessories to build the traces. Full details of the complete range of components and information on where to get them from are published on the 18th of every month in *Sea Angler* magazine.

Mel Russ
Editor, *Sea Angler* magazine

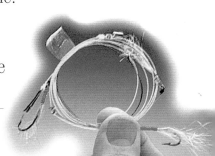

Contents

Catch what's inside...

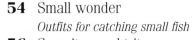

Leaders away!

Are you all fingers and thumbs when it comes to tying a knot? Then you will want to know all about the all-important leader knot

Does the soft pad of your thumb bear scars caused by large, lumpy leader knots slicing across the skin? Is your wallet still recovering from the shock of buying seemingly endless spools of heavy-duty mono following mysterious crack-offs?

Then have no fear! Here we are going to take you through a stage-by-stage, easy to follow sequence on how to tie that all-important leader knot. The 14 close-up shots clearly show you how to tie the most important knot you will ever need to use on the beach.

▼ *Closeup of picture number 8 in the sequence at right. Note how you make turns inside the knot.*

HALF-HITCH PLUS GRINNER

The knot shown in these photographs comprises a simple half-hitch in the leader, with the mainline used to make a four-turn Grinner knot around the leader.

The only tools you are likely to need are pliers, a pair of clippers and a plentiful supply of spittle. First though, what is a leader and why do we need to use one in the first place?

With the power generated by modern rods, coupled to modern casting styles, the line between lead and reel has to cope with some serious pressure. And that's why you need a shockleader (remember the old maxim for leader strength – 10lb of breaking strain for every ounce of lead to be cast) – to be tied in between the main fishing line and the lead.

And to tie a reliable knot that links the thick leader, or shock absorber line, to the thinner main fishing line, you need a special, no-nonsense knot.

Now read on to see how to tie a simple, reliable, compact knot that won't jam in your reel's level-wind, or cut deep into unsuspecting skin.

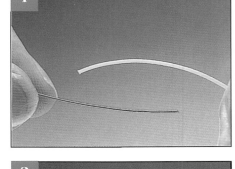

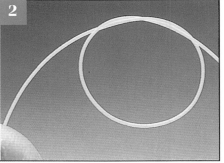

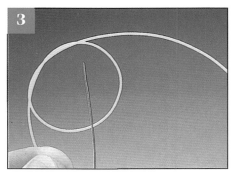

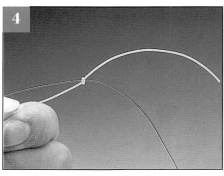

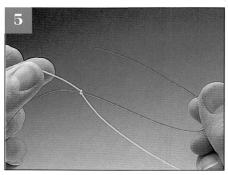

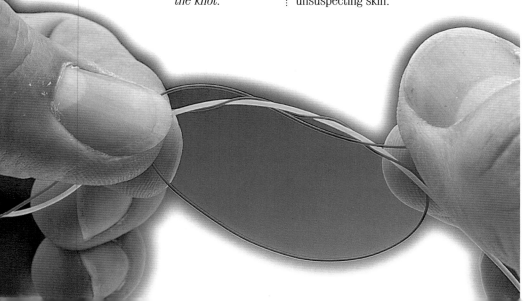

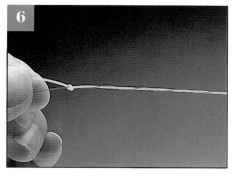

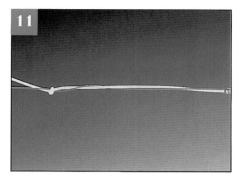

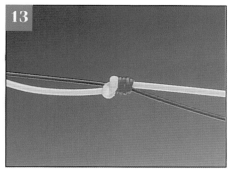

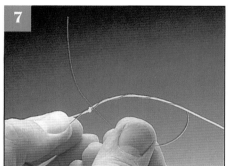

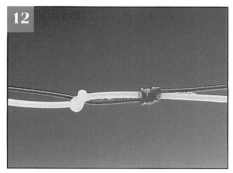

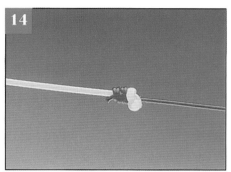

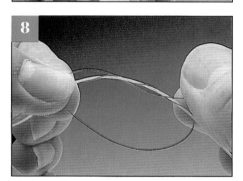

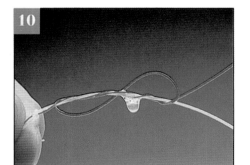

SIMPLE STEP-BY-STEP GUIDE

1 These are the two lines we will be joining, 60lb Siglon and 18lb red Sylcast.

2 First of all tie a single half-hitch in the leader, with a six-inch or so tag.

3 Now push the mainline into the loop. Make sure it goes into the same side of the loop that the tag of the leader comes out.

4 Finger tighten the loop, with a couple of inches of the mainline coming out the other side.

5 Now tighten the loop to pull up the half-hitch. If the tag is too short, use a pair of pliers to pull it through, not forgetting a bit of spit to ease things along. This mainline will be damaged where the knot has been pulled tight, so pull through at least six inches to ensure the weak part is well clear of the finished knot.

6 With the mainline, make four turns around the leader.

7 Bring the mainline tag back and make a loop.

8 Start making turns inside the loop.

9 The full compliment of a further four turns, inside the loop.

10 Before snugging up, coat the loops with a generous helping of lubricant. That's a nice way of saying saliva.

11 Hold the leader tag and mainline and partially tighten the Grinner by pulling the mainline tag. The Grinner will slide up the leader, away from the half-hitch.

12 Add more lubricant to the leader between the two knots and ease the Grinner down to the half-hitch in the leader. Once the two knots are within an eighth-of-an-inch of one another, add yet more lubricant and continue to tighten the Grinner. This is best done by holding the knot between thumb and forefinger and pulling on the mainline through the half-hitch.

13 Once tight, ease the two knots together and fully tighten.

14 Finally trim the tag ends as close as possible.

UNDERSTANDING LEADER DIAMETERS

Typical leaders of 50lb to 60lb breaking strain are between 0.70mm to 0.85mm diameter, whereas 12lb to 18lb mainline is 0.32mm to 0.40mm diameter.

Try a two-hook rig

We start off this section on rig building by explaining how to make a pair of two-hook paternosters

Part of the enjoyment of fishing is making bits and pieces of gear yourself. Many anglers mould their own leads, whip rod rings on bare blanks or dig bait whenever possible, but most spend more time making traces than anything else.

Over the following pages we show you how to make a whole series of end rigs that catch fish. As well as the basic components, we advise on line strengths, hook sizes, snood lengths, etc, to suit as many venues and applications as possible.

So you've decided you want to make your own traces, but where do you get all the bits and pieces – swivels, links, beads, crimps, sequins, hooks, line and cutters? We have used the Docwra Uni-Trace system for this feature, although most tackle shops stock the sort of kit you need.

TOOLS TO USE

While not absolutely necessary, these tools make assembly a lot easier. Clamp a small vice on a flat piece of wood or worktop, with a wire bent as shown, to hold the top swivel in place. Everything can be kept taut and you have something to pull knots up on. Other tools include a Stanley knife blade, long-nose pliers, crimping pliers, nail clippers and a ruler.

COMPONENTS YOU NEED

In this section we will be making two, simple, unclipped traces - one-up, one-down and two-up.
There are times when fish respond better to a hook below the lead; with one-up, one-down, you can cover both options. If fish are coming mostly to the top hook on the one-up, one-downer, switch to this version.

Hooks: They are ideal for dab, flounder, whiting, etc with size 4, 3, 2 or 1, fine to medium-wire hooks, but for larger fish such as coalfish, codling, etc,

▼ *Photos show components for the one-up, one-down rig (top). Note different sequins used on the two-up rig (bottom).*

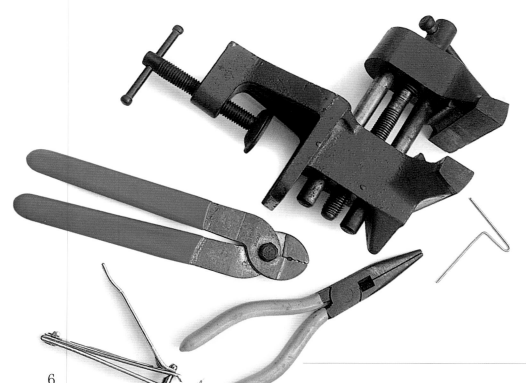

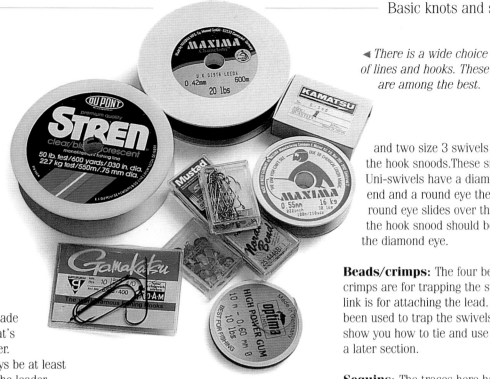

◄ There is a wide choice of lines and hooks. These are among the best.

go up to a size 1, 1/0 or even a 2/0. Suitable hook patterns include Nordic bends, Sea Match blues, Aberdeens, Mustad 3261 and 32613, Kamasan B940, Spearpoints, etc.

Trace: The trace body is made from 50lb or 60lb mono, that's 0.70mm to 0.75mm diameter. The trace body should always be at least equal in breaking strain to the leader, preferably a little stronger. Use 50lb white Stren, which is about 0.73mm, for unclipped traces that will not be blasted to the horizon. Shown here is 60lb Siglon, because it is more photogenic.

Snoods: This line can be anything from 18lb (0.40mm) to 25lb (0.50mm), depending on venue conditions and species. Use the lighter strain over clean ground, stepping up diameter over heavier ground or rougher conditions. These rigs are not really suitable for use over rough, rocky ground, where a rotten-bottom may be more suitable. Avoid bright lines for hook snoods. Try Chameleon or Gantel for general daytime use and Chameleon or black Amnesia after dark. It may not affect the fish, many

anglers do not feel confident using bright orange, fluoro-yellow or pink snoods. Here we have used 20lb Maxima Chameleon and hooks are size 2 Mustad 3261.

Swivels: The two pictures at bottom right on the opposite page show the components required for each of the two rigs. There is one size 1 swivel for the top of the trace

and two size 3 swivels for attaching the hook snoods. These smaller, size 3 Uni-swivels have a diamond eye one end and a round eye the other. The round eye slides over the trace and the hook snood should be attached to the diamond eye.

Beads/crimps: The four beads and four crimps are for trapping the swivels and the link is for attaching the lead. Crimps have been used to trap the swivels, but we will show you how to tie and use stop knots in a later section.

Sequins: The traces here have sequins, but these can be considered as an optional extra. Of the two traces, the silver sequins are used on the one-up, one-down rig. In other words, one hook hangs above the lead and one hangs below. The red sequins are for the trace with both hooks hanging above the lead.

Step-by-step instructions on next page ►

▶ *A group of components from the Dave Docrwa system, top quality equipment that's also neatly packaged and competitively priced.*

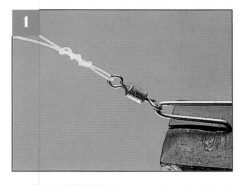

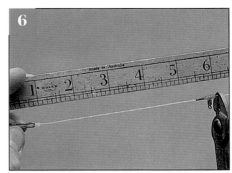

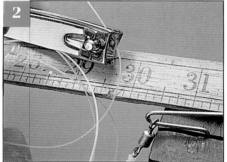

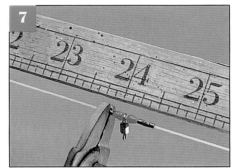

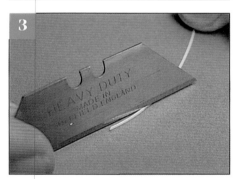

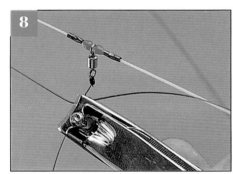

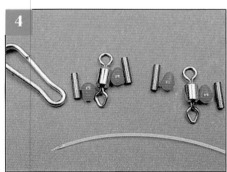

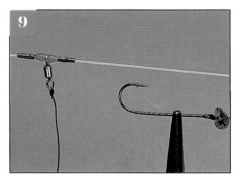

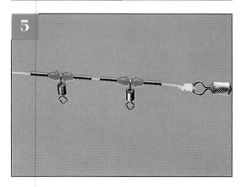

STEP-BY-STEP

In brief...

1   Tying the swivel to the trace head.
2   Cutting the trace body to length.
3   Trimming the end to a fine point.
4   The bits and pieces, ready to slide on.
5   With everything on tie on the lead link.
6   Positioning the lower swivel.
7   Positioning the upper swivel.
8   Cutting hook snood to length.
9   Hook clears swivel, avoiding tangles.
10 Use 12in and 27in on the two-up.

...and in full detail

◆   Firstly, tie the top swivel to the end of the line being used for the trace body, using the trusty grinner knot. Not forgetting a bit of spit to lubricate the line, pull up tight on the wire in the vice.

◆   Next measure the amount of line needed for the body, in this case 36 inches, then add six inches to allow for the link knot, making a total of 42in. For the two-up rig you require 42in for the body, plus 6in for the knot, making a total of 48in.

◆   Cut to length with the nail clippers. It's easier to slide the components on the trace, especially the crimps, if you trim the end of the line to a fine point with a blade.

◆   Once the components are slid on, tie the lead link to the other end of the trace.

◆   You now have a length of heavy line with a swivel one end and a link at the other, with four crimps, four beads and two small swivels between them. With the swivel on the wire in the vice, hold the link level with the ruler's end and pull up tight.

◆   With your free hand, adjust the swivels and stops to the right spacings and tighten the stops with the crimping pliers – use proper crimping pliers, not ordinary pliers.

◆   Once all four crimps have been nipped up with a single pinch, roughly in the middle, tie the snood line to the swivels. Again, use a grinner knot and make sure you are tying it to the diamond eye.

◆   When cutting the snoods to length, keep everything tight and pull the end of the snood to the nearest swivel and cut. Once the hook is tied, the snood will be too short to reach the swivel and there will be nothing for the hook to get tangled on. If you are intending to use sequins, make sure you slip them on the snood before tying the hook.

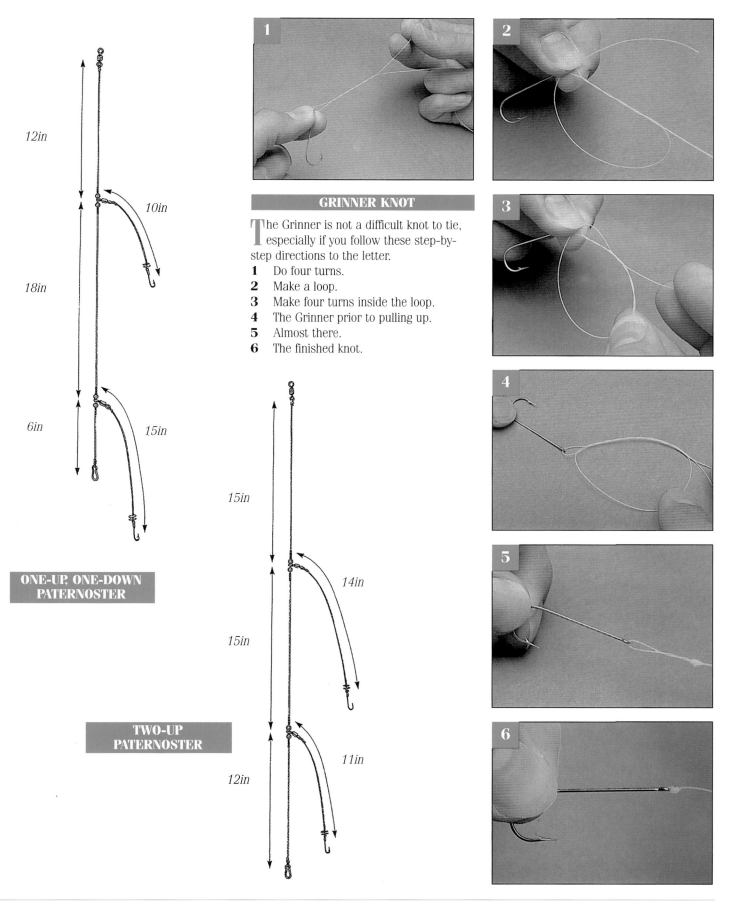

GRINNER KNOT

The Grinner is not a difficult knot to tie, especially if you follow these step-by-step directions to the letter.

1 Do four turns.
2 Make a loop.
3 Make four turns inside the loop.
4 The Grinner prior to pulling up.
5 Almost there.
6 The finished knot.

12in

10in

18in

6in

15in

ONE-UP, ONE-DOWN PATERNOSTER

15in

14in

15in

TWO-UP PATERNOSTER

12in

11in

Going for distance

Successful long-range fishing is the aim with the rigs shown on the next four pages

The debate for and against bait clips will continue to rage. It is a fact, however, that if you want to fish at extreme range, and require your baits to arrive on the sea bed in reasonable shape, then you have to stop them flapping around. And this is where the bait clips come into play...

COMPONENTS AND TOOLS

We have used more components from Dave Docwra's Uni-Trace system, plus sequins and a Breakaway Impact Shield. The main trace body is Siglon as it shows up clearly in photographs. Although it is fine for leaders, many anglers choose a more subtle colour, such as 60lb Maxima or 60lb Docwra C26.

This is a clipped trace that will see some serious casting, so the body should be made of a quality mono. Use a minimum 0.75mm diameter, around 60lb breaking strain. Hook snoods are 23lb Maxima Chameleon and the stop knots are tied from 0.60mm diameter, 11lb Power Gum.

Tools we used include a vice and length of bent wire, ruler, crimping pliers, long-nosed pliers, nail clippers and a Stanley knife blade. Leeda's Fishin' Glue was used for the main knots because it is formulated for mono line and retains some flexibility even when cured.

TWO HOOKS CLIPPED UP

The first trace is a two-hook, clipped up rig using standard wire clips. With the hooks being clipped up, there's no need to put any bait stops or sequins on the snoods. Don't forget that air pressure will make sure that the bait stays at the hook end of the snood during the cast.

Use this rig when you cannot cast an unclipped trace far enough or cannot retain good bait presentation. It is designed for distance casting for any species, but generally catches, whiting, codling, dab and occasionally flounder if you land on mud.

Hooks are size 1 Kamasan B940. I tend to use size 2 on my unclipped traces, with size 1 on a clipped rig because of the extra strength and security they offer when winding in over a greater distance.

TWO HOOKS STEP-BY-STEP

1 Components include a size 1 swivel for the trace top, two size 3 swivels for the snoods, four Aero beads and crimps to trap the snood swivels, a Uni-link for the sinker.
2 Once the swivel has been tied to the head of the trace, cut the line to length, adding six inches for the link knot. Slide on components in the right order, tie on the link at the end.

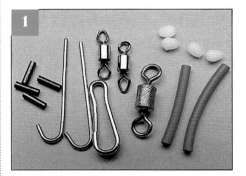

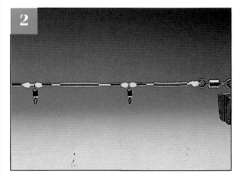

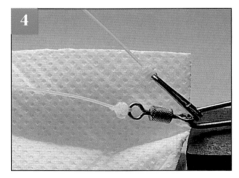

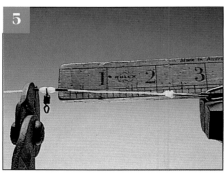

TYING THE STOP KNOT

When used as a stop knot on mono, Power Gum is slightly stretchy and rubbery to touch, creating a strong grip in a few seconds. Once the seal is broken and the area moistened with saliva, it slides easily until left in one place again, making it ideal for semi-permanent stops.

STEP-BY-STEP

1 Keep the line to which the stop knot is being tied tight. Hold the PG against the mono with 75mm or so protruding.

2 Make four turns of Power Gum around the mono.

3 Bring back the end of the line to form a loop.

4 Make four more turns inside the loop and pull up loosely. Moisten, pull up tightly but do not over tighten, move to final position and trim ends.

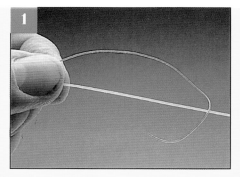
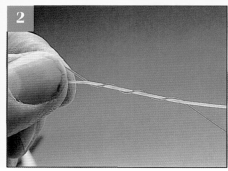
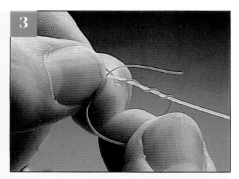
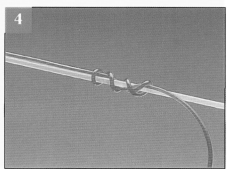

3 Add a drop of Superglue on the two main knots at the top and bottom of the rig.

4 Just put a single drop on the knot, then remove surplus glue immediately by pinching between several layers of tissue.

5 Once the glue has dried, stretch out the trace and with a ruler, position the swivels and crimps in place, then tighten the crimps with a pair of crimping pliers.

6 Slide the wire part of the bait clips into the plastic sleeve. It's best with the sleeve in its final position – sliding it around too much can loosen its grip on the line. Round off the clip's end to avoid sharp edges.

7 Once the wire is all the way through, with 5mm protruding, bend the last 3mm or so up at right angles. This stops the wire pulling out of the sleeve during the cast.

8 The finished bait clip for the lower snood in position, about 15mm below the upper snood swivel.

9 The snood has been tied to the swivel and cut to length. 10mm further up the trace than the end of the clip. Slide a 40mm length of Uni-tube on to the snood then tie on the hook to prevent tangles and improve presentation.

Step-by-step continued next page ▶

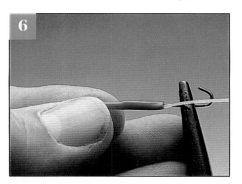
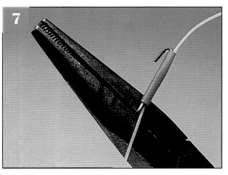
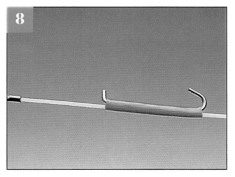
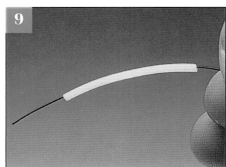

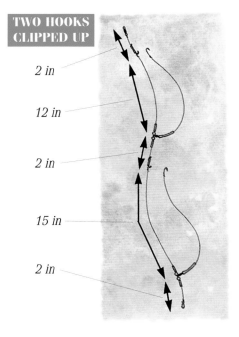

TWO HOOKS CLIPPED UP

2 in

12 in

2 in

15 in

2 in

10 Once the hook has been attached, the tube is pushed over the knot and just on to the diamond eye of the swivel.

11 With the hooks attached, it is now time to make the final adjustments to the bait clips. Once everything is in position, tie a Power Gum stop knot 10mm below the clip. This will stop the clip sliding too far during the cast and make repositioning easier for the next cast.

12 A selection of finished articles.

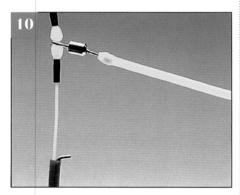

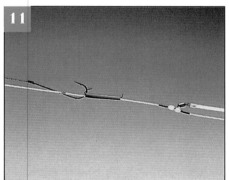

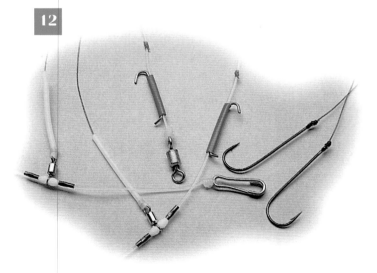

▲ *Components for the Two Hooks, Clipped Down rig include a size 1 swivel, two size 3 swivels, four Aero beads, crimps, Uni link, Impact Shield, bead and crimp, two sequins per snood and a micro bead between sequin and stop knot.*

TWO-HOOKS, CLIPPED DOWN

This trace has the hooks clipped down. Sequins have been added as bait stops to prevent the baits sliding up the line. For improved aerodynamics, replace the lower bait clip with a Breakaway Impact Shield. It has similar uses to the previous rig, but is capable of placing presentable baits at a greater range.

With a view to quality fish, such as bigger whiting and codling, often found at range among banks and gullies, use size 1, 79515 Viking hooks. Their design gives you a greater chance of landing a better fish at long range.

SIMPLE STEP-BY-STEP

1 Place all the goodies on the trace body and tie the link on. Remember that without the bead and crimp above the Impact Shield, it won't work.

2 As this is another distance trace, the main knots are given a drop of Superglue. Remove

surplus glue immediately with a tissue. This prevents the line oxidising and weakening. Never forget that keeping Superglue off your flesh is essential – only nail polish remover has any chance of removing it once it has set firm.

3 The Impact Shield is held in place by carefully pushing the foot into a piece of rubber tube.

4 With one end of the trace held firmly by the wire hook in the vice, components are slid gently into position and the crimps are fastened with the crimping pliers – don't forget to use these tools, not a pair of ordinary pliers.

5 Once the swivels are fixed in place, slide the wire bait clip into the plastic sheath and turn up one end to prevent the wire pulling out.

6 With all the bits and pieces where they should be, tie on the snood mono and cut to length. This should be 10mm or so past the bait clip, to allow for tying the hook to the snood.

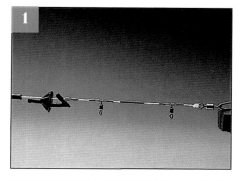

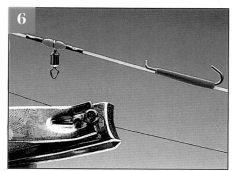

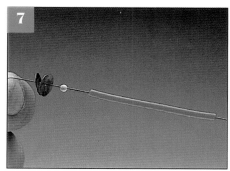

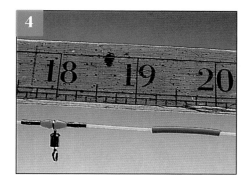

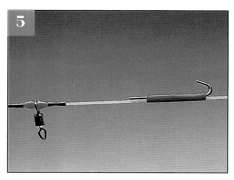

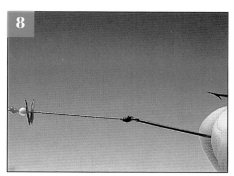

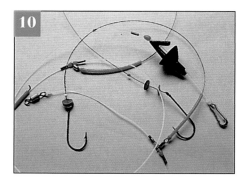

7 We are using Uni-tube, again to enhance presentation. Slide on 40mm or so, then the micro bead, and finally add the two sequins.

8 Here the hook has been attached and the sequin bait stop is held 50mm or so above the hook by a Power Gum stop knot.

9 Once snoods, hooks, etc, are tied, stretch out the rig and make the final adjustments to the clips. When everything is in place, fasten the crimp above the Impact Shield to allow 3mm between shield and bead. Use a Power Gum stop knot above the top bait clip to stop it sliding too far during the cast.

10 The end product, a two-hook clipped distance trace with bait stops.

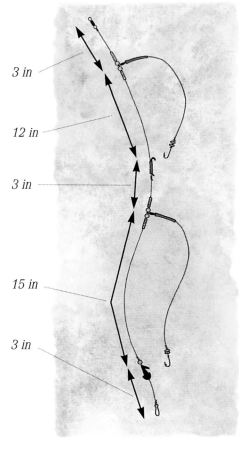

3 in

12 in

3 in

15 in

3 in

**TWO HOOKS
CLIPPED
DOWN**

Tie a plaice trace

Spring is the time to set your stall out to catch a plaice, those plate-size flatties that sport bright orange spots across their backs

Plaice are predominantly sight feeders, so anglers get the chance to bring out all those colourful beads and sequins to try and attract their attention.

The two traces demonstrated here both employ bright attractor beads and sequins above size 1 Mustad 3261 Aberdeen hooks. Common baits are lugworm or ragworm, made more attractive with very thin strips of white squid flash.

COMPONENTS AND TOOLS

We used Dave Docwra's Uni-trace system, plus sequins, beads and a Breakaway Impact Shield. Tools include a vice, length of bent wire, a ruler, crimping pliers, long-nosed pliers, nail clippers and a Stanley knife blade. The trace body is 60lb Siglon for clarity in the photos, but for fishing use quality mono, with a minimum 0.75mm diameter/60lb breaking strain. The hook snoods can be 20lb to 25lb Maxima Chameleon, while the top knots are tied from 0.60mm diameter/1lb Power Gum.

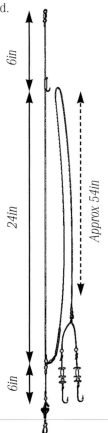

SINGLE HOOK UP AND DOWN

SINGLE HOOK WITH LONG TRACE

This is a single hook rig about 36in long, with the snood six inches up from the lead. It includes a long 54in hooklength to give a more natural bait presentation, which would be almost impossible to cast any distance if it wasn't doubled back and clipped down.

We have solved the problem by attaching a second bait clip at the top of the trace, so the line goes up and round the top clip, then down to the lower clip, in this case an Impact Shield.

SIMPLE STEP-BY-STEP

1 Components are standard for a single snood rig - size 1 swivel for the top of the trace, size 3 swivel for the snood. Aerobeads and crimps for trapping the snood swivel and a Uni-link for the sinker. Additional units include a standard bait clip at the top, lower Impact Shield and a variety of beads and sequins as attractors.

2 Tie the top swivel to the body material using a Grinner knot. Here we have used Knot Ease, instead of saliva, to lubricate the main knots as they are pulled up.

3 The trace body should be about 36in long, so once the top swivel is tied, add 6in before cutting to length to allow for the bottom knot.

4 To help thread the components on the trace body, chamfer the other end of the trace with a knife blade. Now slide all the components on, making sure they are in the right order, then tie on the lead link.

5 For distance traces, use Superglue on the main knots at the top and bottom of the rig adds security. Put one drop on the knot then pinch between several layers of tissue to remove all but a trace of glue.

6 Slide the wire part of the bait clip into the plastic sleeve. This is best done with

the clip near its final position, 6in or so from the trace top. Round off the clip's end, so sharp edges do not damage the line.

7 Once the wire is through, with about 5mm protruding, bend the last 3mm or so up at right angles. This stops the wire pulling out of the sleeve during the cast.

8 Using the ruler, position the snood swivel, beads and crimps with the Impact Shield half-an-inch above the lead link.

9 Once everything is in place, apply light pressure to the crimps, using proper pliers.

10 Using the trusty Grinner knot, tie the snood line, which is 25lb Maxima, to the swivel but do not cut to length yet.

11 Take the line up to the top bait clip.

12 Then take it back down to the Impact Shield and cut to length.

13 Now slide on a short piece of Uni-tube, plus beads and sequin attractors.

14 The Uni-tube helps stop the long snood tangling, by making it stand out from the trace body. Colour is down to you. Try using something less colourful, so as not to detract from the attractors near the hook.

15 Once the hook has been tied on, you will need a stop knot above the attractors to keep them close to the bait. Power Gum is ideal, as it can be moved around; with care, it will not damage the snood.

16 The finished article, with the snood going up to and over the top clip, then down to the Impact Shield.

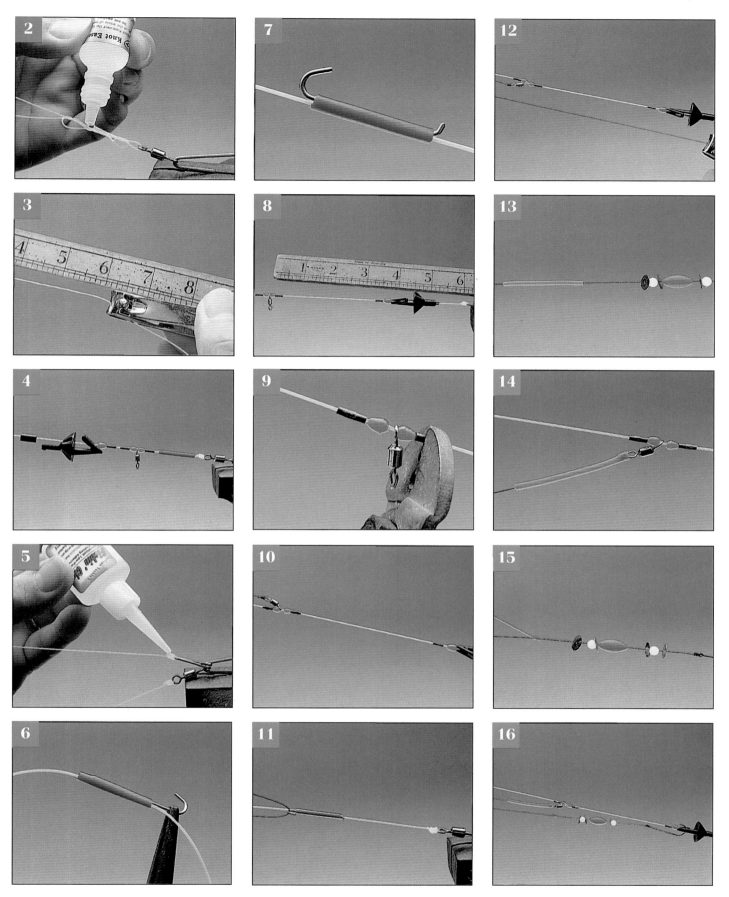

TRACE STORAGE

So you have made all your traces, but how will you keep them neat and tidy to stop them tangling? The best way is to coil up each rig and store it in a proper trace wallet. It is not foolproof, but near enough.

SIMPLE STEP-BY-STEP

A Use Sellotape, garden ties or a pipe cleaner to keep it all neat and tidy

B A neatly-coiled trace ready for tying together

C Held with Sellotape, a note is added, containing all the key details of rig identification

D A garden tie or pipe cleaner can be used to hold the trace

E Ready to use – all coiled up in the wallet with the label showing clearly

SLIDING WISHBONE

This second attractor-type trace is a clipped two-hooker with both hooks held by one clip. Often called a sliding Wishbone, it will cast a good distance and present two, separate baits.

SIMPLE STEP-BY-STEP

1 The essentials are: size 1 and 3 swivels, Aerobeads, crimps, Impact Shield, attractor beads and sequins, plus a length of Uni-tube.

2 Straight in with a Grinner to attach the top swivel. The trace is going to be about 36in long, so add 6in to allow for the lower knot and cut to length.

3 Before sliding the components on, especially the crimps, chamfer the cut end with a sharp blade.

4 All the bits and pieces in the right order. Once the lead link is tied on, now is the time to put a drop of Superglue on the two main knots.

5 Use the rule to position the snood swivel, beads and the crimps.

6 Tighten the crimps with crimping pliers. Note that because positioning is critical, you could leave the final positioning of this component until the end.

7 Now tie on the snood material, which in this case is 30lb Maxima. This is thicker than normal, to avoid tangles.

8 The swivel for the sliding part of the Wishbone should be about 10in above the Impact Shield. Overall trace dimensions are not critical, but this part is, so measure down from the snood swivel to 10in above the Impact Shield; then add 3in or so for the knot and cut.

9 With the swivel tied to the end of the snood, it should sit about 10in above the Breakaway Impact Shield.

10 This part can get rather complicated, so take it slowly and carefully. Cut about 30in of 23lb line and tie one of the hooks to an end.

Thread on the attractors and a small bead, then thread the end of the line through the lower snood swivel. Now thread on another small bead, followed by the attractors. With the swivel 10in above the Shield, the length of this line should be twice that (20in). So measure off 20in, then add 3in cut and tie on the second hook.

11 A stop knot is needed now, both as a bait stop and so that if a fish is hooked, the other hook will still fish. Using Power Gum, tie a stop knot between the small bead and top attractor for both hooks.

12 Now make sure both hooks will fit tightly on the Impact Shield.

13 Tighten the crimp above the Shield stop bead.

14 This is the optional piece of Uni-tube that can be put over the top snood to help prevent the finished item from getting tangled up.

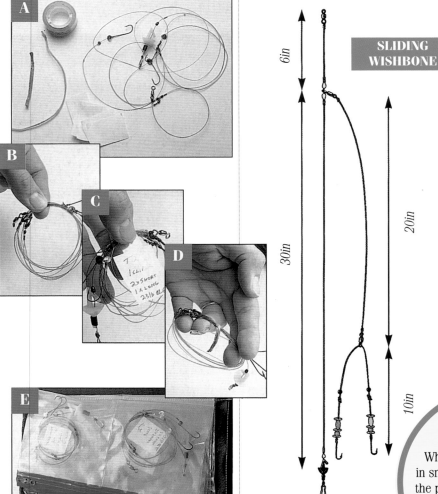

SLIDING WISHBONE

6in
30in
20in
10in

TRIAL AND ERROR

When you tie a Grinner knot in snood line, it usually reduces the pre-cut length by about 3in. It's really a case of trial and error. Try a few dummies first to see how it ties together.

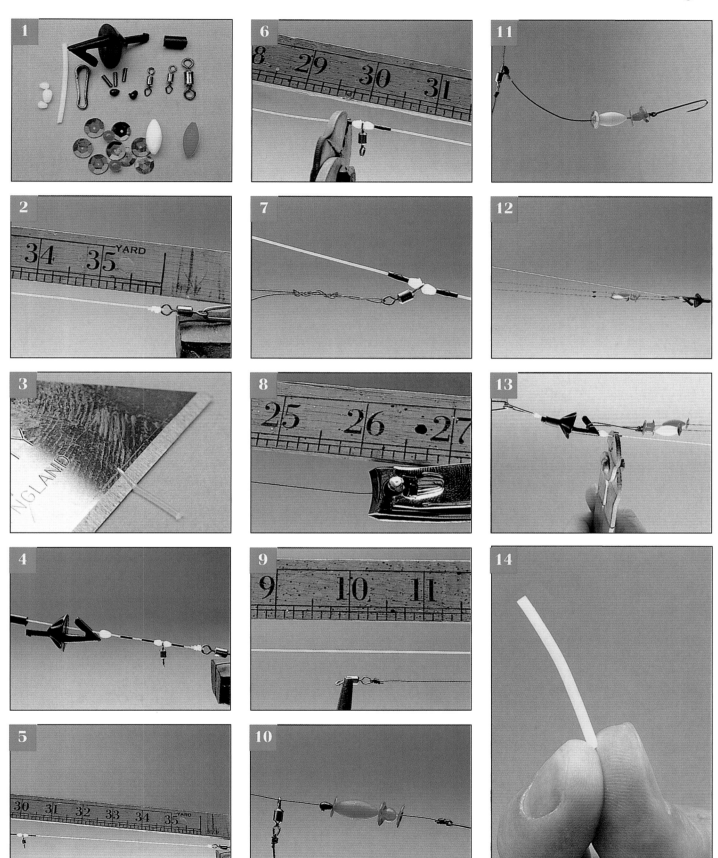

Make yours a double

These are double-hook rigs with a difference!

Two hooks in one bait, or a pair together with two baits, are common methods of putting out a large scent trail. The first is called a Pennell, the second a Wishbone. The Wishbone has two separate short hook lengths lying side by side, while the Pennell is armed with two hooks, one tied just above the other to give greater hooking power. Our two traces show both types on a single snood trace incorporating a Breakaway Impact Shield for maximum distance and minimum bait disruption.

COMPONENTS AND TOOLS

Main components are again from Dave Docwra's Uni-trace system, plus the all important Impact Shield from Breakaway.

Main tools are a vice, a piece of bent wire and an 18in plastic ruler. Crimping pliers, long-nosed pliers, nail clippers and a Stanley knife blade complete the kit.

Trace body material is 60lb Siglon, but whatever you use go for a quality mono, minimum 0.75mm diameter/60lb breaking strain for angling.

Hook snoods are 25lb Maxima Chameleon and the stop knots are tied from 0.60mm diameter/11lb Power Gum. Hooks are two size 1/0 Mustad 32813 worm hooks and two size 1 Aberdeens.

WISHBONE RIG

First of these double-hook rigs on the workbench is the Wishbone, which is easy enough to tie if you know exactly how, but a real nightmare job if you don't. The beauty of the Wishbone is two-fold: you can present two similar baits next to one another, or two different types to increase the scent trail.

For instance, two large, freshout black lugworm side by side make a tempting offering for a hungry cod or bass, while a freshout on one hook and a white ragworm or three razorfish on the other will make the ideal cocktail.

Both of these methods make it possible to present a large bait or a cocktail with

WISHBONE RIG

12in

18in

12in

6in

WISHBONE RIG

little fear of masking the points. This means that you do not need huge hooks, which in this instance are size 1/0, 3261 chemically-etched Aberdeens.

BUILDING THE BASIC TRACE

1 The hardware you need for success: top swivel, link, snood swivel, Aerobead, Uni-tube, crimps and an Impact Shield, plus a couple of hooks.
2 The top swivel is attached, via a universal Grinner knot.
3 The trace should be about 30in long, so again, double up, with the help of the 18in rule, which includes 6in allowed for the link knot.
4 Cut the nylon at an angle to make threading on all the various the components easier.
5 Is everything in its correct place? Then tie on the lead link.
6 See *Tying the Wishbone* 6a-6h below.
7 Thread the Uni-tube on to the snood and tie to the snood swivel.
8 Slide the Uni-tube up to and over knot.
9 With the lead link held firmly, place the hooks in the Impact Shield and position the snood swivel.
10 With everything in place, tighten the crimps either side of the snood swivel to produce a long-range Wishbone.

TYING THE WISHBONE

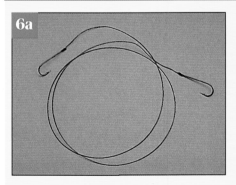

6a

Follow these simple step-by-step instructions to make sure sure you get this most important element of your rig completely ship-shape.

6a The secret of success is to tie both hooks first and then tie the knot above the hooks. The snood wants to end up about

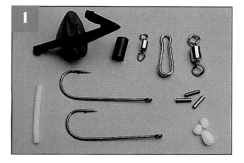

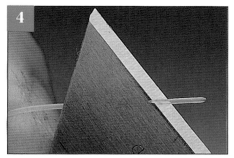

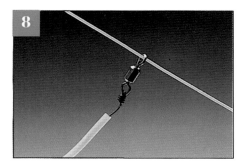

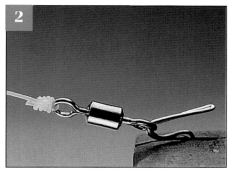

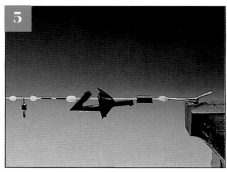

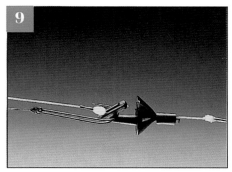

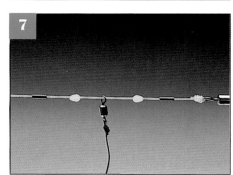

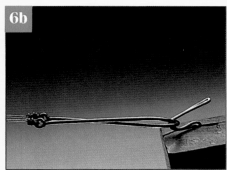

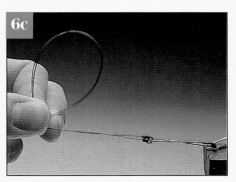

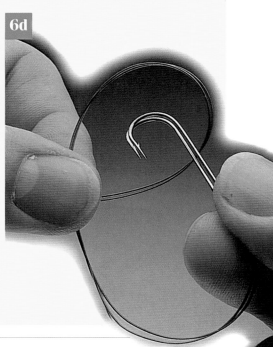

18 inches long, therefore cut an initial length of about 36 inches and then tie a hook to each end.

6b Place both hooks on the vice clip.

6c This knot is called a water knot. It is used by fly-anglers to add a dropper, or second fly above the main on; it is also an ideal knot for a Wishbone. With the hooks

in the wire grip, make a 3in diameter loop in the doubled snood line, 3in or 4in above the hooks.

6d Holding the loop, remove hooks from the wire grip and keeping the hooks together, pass through loop.

Continued next page ▶

TIEING THE WISHBONE *Continued*

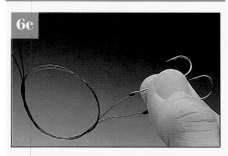

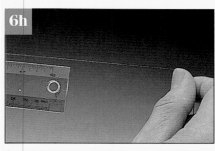

6e Make two more passes with the hooks, so they have gone through the loop three times – each of them in the same direction, of course.

6f Place hooks back in the wire grip, moisten loose knot, work into position to give the correct length from knot to hook.

6g Pull up, teasing the coils together before finally tightening.

6h With the Wishbone tied, cut the overall snood to length, plus the knot allowance. We want an 18in snood, so add 3in or so for the top knot and cut.

◄ *Now return to* **picture 7** *in the main step-by-step sequence on previous page.*

CLIPPED-DOWN PENNELL

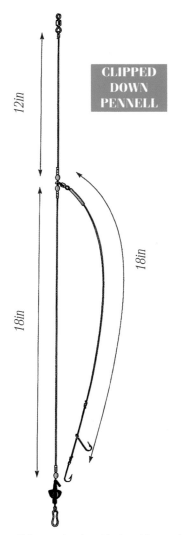

CLIPPED DOWN PENNELL

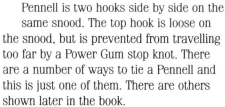

Pennell is two hooks side by side on the same snood. The top hook is loose on the snood, but is prevented from travelling too far by a Power Gum stop knot. There are a number of ways to tie a Pennell and this is just one of them. There are others shown later in the book.

An Impact Shield is used here in place of a conventional bait clip. It is, of course, suitable for most fish, and it works best with worm baits, where the length of the bait varies.

With whiting around, it is not uncommon to have a fish on each hook. Indeed, when small codling are near the beach in numbers, they have been known to come in two at a time on a Pennell. Hooks in this case are size 1/0, 32813.

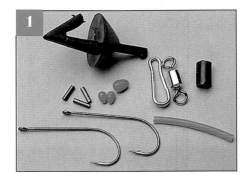

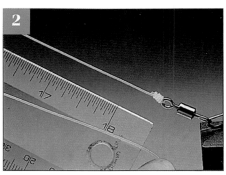

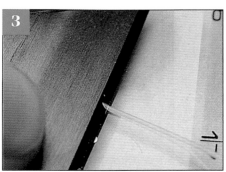

SIMPLE STEP-BY-STEP

1 Components, including top swivel, lead link, Impact Shield, beads, Uni-tube, crimps and a pair of hooks. The eagle-eyed will have noticed we have accidentally omitted the snood swivel.

2 With the top swivel tied on, it is time to measure the body. This is an 18in rule, so for this 30in trace, double the line and include 6in or so for the link knot.

3 Chamfer the end of the line with a Stanley knife blade to make it easier to thread all the components on the body.

4 Now is the time to check that everything is in the right order and the tie is on the lead link.

5 For extra security, now add a small dob of Superglue, wiping the excess carefully off with tissues.

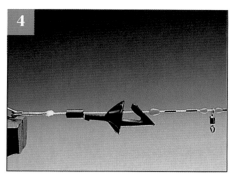

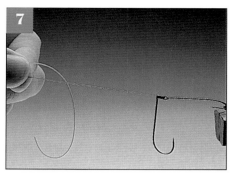

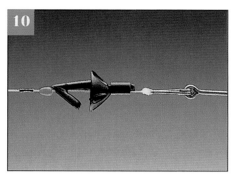

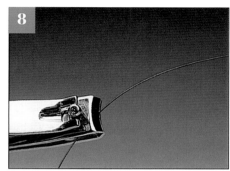

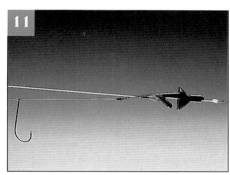

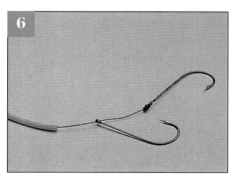

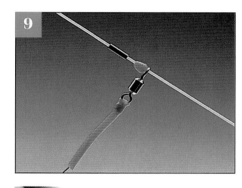

6 The snood, with the lower hook tied on with the trusty Grinner knot, the second hook and Uni-tube loose.

7 Tie a Power Gum stop knot to prevent the top hook moving up the snood.

8 Trim snood to length, before tying to snood swivel, allowing 3in for the knot.

9 Once tied, slide the Uni-tube up and over the knot and half of the swivel eye. This will help prevent the snood tangling.

10 Tighten the crimp a couple of millimetres above the Impact Shield.

11 Stretch out the body and position the snood swivel, beads and the crimps.

12 Now make sure that everything is in the right place and taut – then squeeze those crimps and you have a first-class long-range Pennell rig.

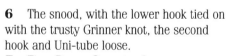

WATCH OUT FOR SUPERGLUE!

We can't say this often enough – be ultra-careful with superglue, and don't slosh the stuff on your fingers. Flesh can be stuck so firmly that it can take a hospital visit to prise things apart.

Float fantastic

Float-fishing offers the sea angler the chance of some fun-tastic sport. Here we show you how to make three types of rigs that are deadly for catching ballan wrasse, pollack, garfish and mackerel from rocks, harbour walls and piers

There are few more pleasant and rewarding ways of catching fast-running summer species than on light float tackle. Mackerel six at a time on feathers can hardly be described as sport, but a 1lb mackerel on a spinning rod and float certainly can be.

A tail-walking garfish is as close as many UK anglers will ever get to game fishing, while a 2lb pollack hitting a head-hooked king ragworm suspended below a float will really get the adrenaline pumping.

A spinning or carp-type rod, medium fixed-spool reel loaded with 8lb to 12lb line and a float that will support up to an ounce or so of lead is the ideal gear for tackling summer rock marks. Mackerel, garfish, pollack, scad, mullet, coalfish, bass, wrasse, even some flatfish will take a bait suspended from a float.

There are many ways to rig a float, and here we spotlight perhaps the most popular methods. The first is ideal for casting a good distance, especially from the beach, where garfish, mackerel and bass are patrolling behind the breakers for sandeel and whitebait. The second is a conventional sliding float rig, and lastly a variation of the sliding float, utilising a leadhead.

COMPONENTS YOU NEED

Pictured here are all the components required for making the floats described in this section.

A A selection of sliding floats. In all cases, the line slides through a central hole.
B Weights, bullets and barrels - for cocking the float.
C Hooks for floatfishing. Fine-wire for good penetration in hard, bony mouths. Short-shank, medium-wire for hard runners like bass and pollack. Stronger heavier wire for wrasse in the rocks. A leadhead is ideal for presenting live sandeel or king rag.
D A hook snood of around 15lb is a good

compromise for toothy specimens and bait presentation. For fishing over rough ground, however, increase the mainline but use a snood with a lower strength so you do not lose the float if the hook snags.

THE CASTING FLOAT

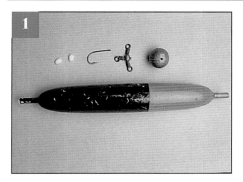

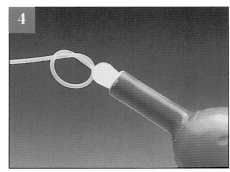

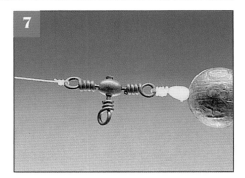

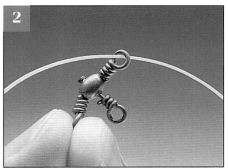

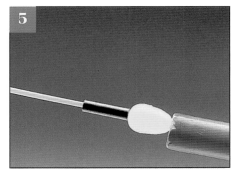

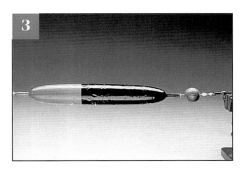

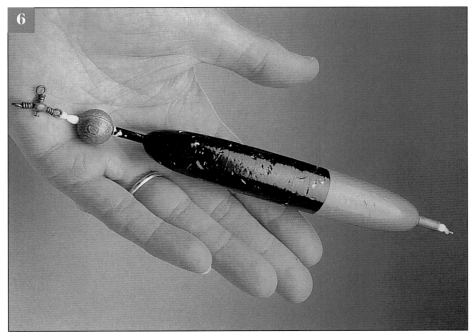

SIMPLE STEP-BY-STEP

1   Here are all the components that you will need for this : a sliding float and a three-way swivel, a hook, weight and a couple of beads.

2   First of all, tie the three-way swivel to a length of at least 50lb mono line, about 18in long.

3   Once the three-way swivel is properly secured, slide all the components carefully on to the monofilament in reverse order, that is – bead, weight, float, followed by another bead.

4   Now tie a half-hitch above the float, sliding it down as close to the bead as possible, before tightening.

5   If you wish, an alternative to using the knot is a crimp.

6   The float is now ready for attaching to the mainline.

7   Now tie the mainline to the opposite eye on the three-way swivel.

8   The hook snood is now tied to the remaining eye of the swivel. Its length can vary from two feet up to eight to ten feet. Remember that the longer the snood, the more difficult it will be to cast and keep the bait intact.

UNIVERSAL SLIDING FLOAT

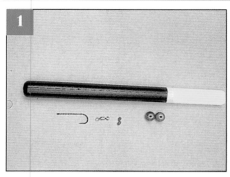

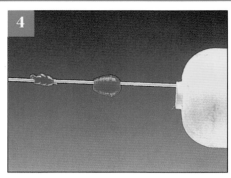

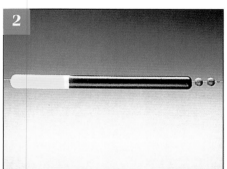

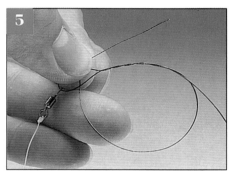

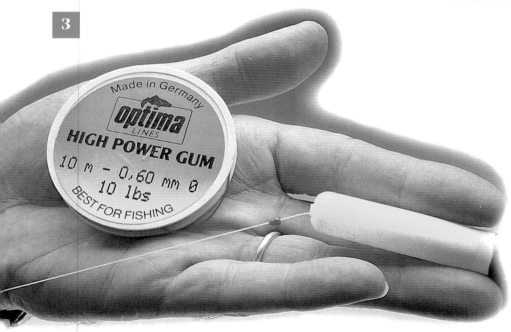

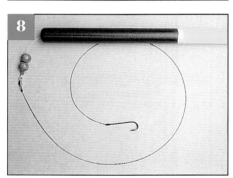

UNIVERSAL
SLIDING
FLOAT

SIMPLE STEP-BY-STEP

1   All the bits and pieces you need to complete the job – sliding float, swivel, hook, weight and a couple of beads.

2   Slide the components carefully onto the mainline, bead, float, weight(s) and bead. This last bead protects the knot from the weights. Now tie on the swivel.

3   Use Powergum to tie a stop knot, which stops the float at the required depth. *See separate sequence on page opposite on tying a stop knot.*

4   The finished knot stops the bead that stops the float which then fishes at the required depth.

5   Tying on the hook snood.

6   This is how the float will sit for casting, right above the weight.

7   The snood can vary in length, depending on fishing conditions, but start off at around 20 inches.

8   The finished rig. Everything is in the right order and the tie is on the lead link.

SLIDING FLOAT WITH LEADHEAD

This has to be one of the easiest items to make in this entire book!

SIMPLE STEP-BY-STEP

1 You need is a float, bead and leadhead!

2 Slide on the bead and float, then tie a leadhead that will cock the float. Simply tie the stop knot at the required depth.

3 That's it: the leadhead holds the hook at right angles, offering better presentation for baits such as live sandeel and ragworm.

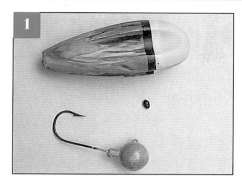

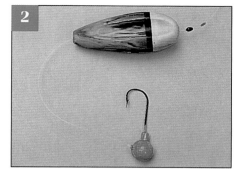

SLIDING FLOAT WITH LEADHEAD

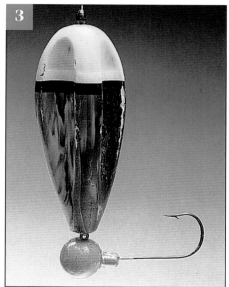

TYING A STOP KNOT

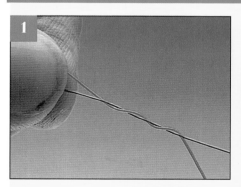

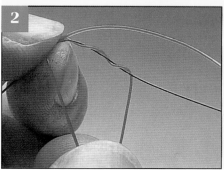

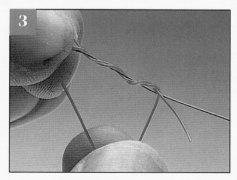

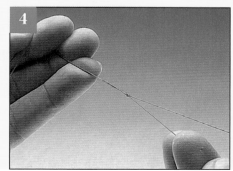

A stop-knot is used to hold accessories on the main trace or snoods. Such knots are often used in place of crimps.

SIMPLE STEP-BY-STEP

1 Keep the mainline tight, hold the Powergum next to the mono, with a tag about 4in or 5in long.

2 With the Powergum, make four turns around the mainline.

3 Now make a loop and make another four turns inside the loop.

4 Pull up almost tight, position and finally tighten.

5 You can use ordinary mono, but remember to use a breaking strain a few pounds lighter than the main line. You need to leave tags 2in or 3in long, which will help prevent it catching on the rod rings.

Fast feathers

An easy guide to making your own mackerel feather traces

Shop-bought traces catch fish, but there's nothing like the added thrill of luring fish on gear you have made yourself. This way you can make them just how you want them and it usually works out a bit cheaper, as well. To make a string of white feathers we have used white cock hackle feathers, available from tackle shops that stock fly-gear.

As an alternative to the hackle feathers, buy a feather duster from a hardware shop. The silver, tinsel-type lures are made from mylar tube, again used in fly-tying, and generally available in gold or silver.

Mackerel feathers come in all shapes and sizes, but to keep things simple we have made two sets of three. A string of six is usually associated with boat fishing, with shore anglers opting for the lighter, and easier to cast, row of three. Many mackerel are wasted because people catch far more than they can actually use.

FEATHER LURE STEP-BY-STEP

1 These are the basic tools and materials you will need. Hooks (size 1, stainless steel O'Shaughnessy), pair of scissors, Stanley knife blade, whipping thread, white feathers, mylar tube and some Superglue.

2 You do not need a special fly tying vice, here we are using an ordinary engineer's vice to hold the hook.

3 Put the end of the thread through the hook eye, then whip halfway down the hook shank. This gives the feather shafts something to grip, rather than sliding around the smooth hook shank when you start to whip them.

4 Take four of five feathers and strip the soft fibres from the butt end of the feather for an inch or so; this makes it easier to whip to the hook shank.

5 Start whipping the butt ends to the hook shank, working up towards the eye.

6 Once the whipping is halfway up, trim the butt ends.

7 Just below the hook eye is ideal.

8 Continue whipping to the hook eye.

9 Keep the thread tight and apply a drop of Superglue to the end. Once set, trim with the Stanley blade.

10 Trim the feathers to length, not too long though, or the fish cannot get the hook in its mouth.

11 Finally, soak the whipping in Superglue, wipe off surplus, allow to dry.

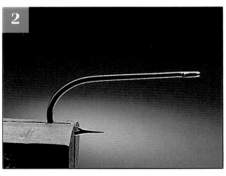

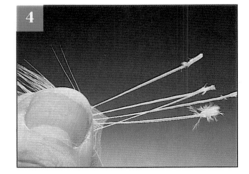

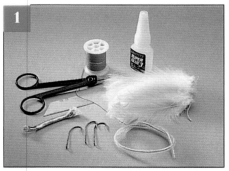

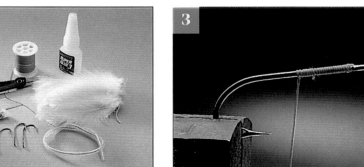

MYLAR LURES

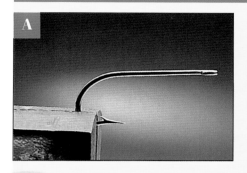

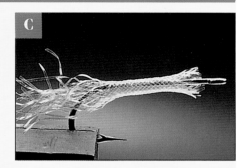

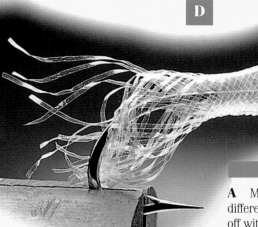

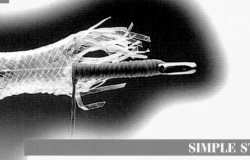

SIMPLE STEP-BY-STEP

A Mylar tube has to be handled slightly differently, but the basics are similar. Start off with the hook in a vice.

B Cut a length of mylar, about 40mm long and tease out one end.

C Slide the length gently over the eye of the hook, making sure that the teased-out end is towards the point.

D Starting at the eye, whip halfway down the shank as before, keeping the mylar out of the way.

E Pull the mylar over the whipping up to just below the eye and start to whip over the mylar back towards the eye.

F Continue whipping up to the hook eye.

Continued next page ▶

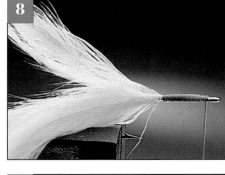

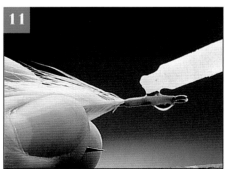

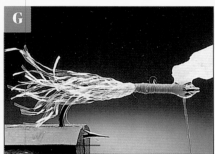

G Hold the thread tight and put a drop of Superglue on the thread end, keeping the thread tight until dry, before trimming with the Stanley knife.
H Superglue the whipping, wipe off the surplus and allow to dry.
I The finished products – three white feathers and three silver mylar lures. As an added attraction, a brightly-coloured bead above the hook often enhances their performance.

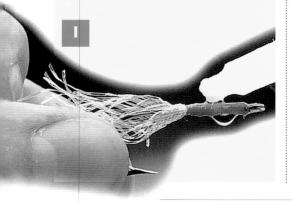

MAKING THE TRACE

Once you have made up your lures and the glue is dry, one of the easiest ways to make a set of three is to use a water knot. This is a knot that is used frequently by fly-anglers to tie on a dropper, or small lure, in addition to the main fly on the end of the line.

SIMPLE STEP-BY-STEP

1 In addition to the lures, you need a swivel, lead link, 50lb or 60lb mono line for the trace body and something like 25lb mono for your hook snoods.
2 Tie the trace body to the leader and trim the knot.
3 We want to end up with a trace about 36in long, so add 12in or so to allow for knots and cut to length.
4 Pull off three 18in lengths of snood line to hold the three lures. Hold a snood length against the trace 6in below the swivel.
5 Make a loop with both lines, using line from below the hold point.
6 Now put the loose ends through the loop and pull through.
7 Take the loose ends through the loop twice more.
8 Keeping the loose ends together, wrap them around your hand and grip the short snood end with pliers. With the swivel firmly on the wire in the vice, pull it all up tight, not forgetting a generous dob of spit to ease the way.
9 Trim the short snood end to within 2mm of the knot. The actual knot has tightened up about 9in down from the swivel, perfect for a three-hooker.
10 Start the next water knot about 6in below the first and repeat the process.
11 With all three snoods tied, trim each one to about 9in long.
12 Slide on the lures, taking the hook half way down the snood and tying with the good old Grinner knot. If your thing is beads, now's the time to slip one on the snood above the hook.
13 Once tied, the hook lies a little under halfway between the two knots. There is no way two lures can tangle unless the trace is allowed to go slack.
14 With the trace now all but complete, it is time to tie on the lead link. The length

has worked out just right, being the desired 36in, plus three inches or so to allow for the knot.
15 This trace will be cast far more than a conventional leger, so a dob of Superglue on the top and bottom knot will add to the safety factor. Do not forget to wipe off the surplus glue with a tissue immediately after it has been applied.
16 The completed trace, to give a clearer view of the spacing. Mackerel tend to swim in tight shoals, so keep them close together.
17 Finally, keep your made-up traces neatly coiled and ready for use. There's nothing worse that trying to untangle a cat's cradle of hooks, nylon and feathers! To stop the coils unravelling, secure them with food bag twists.

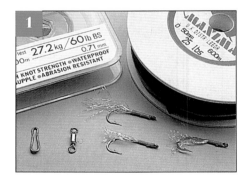

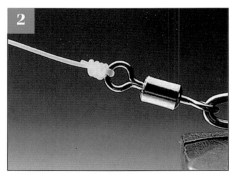

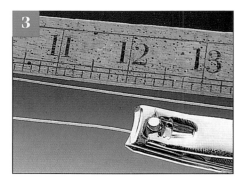

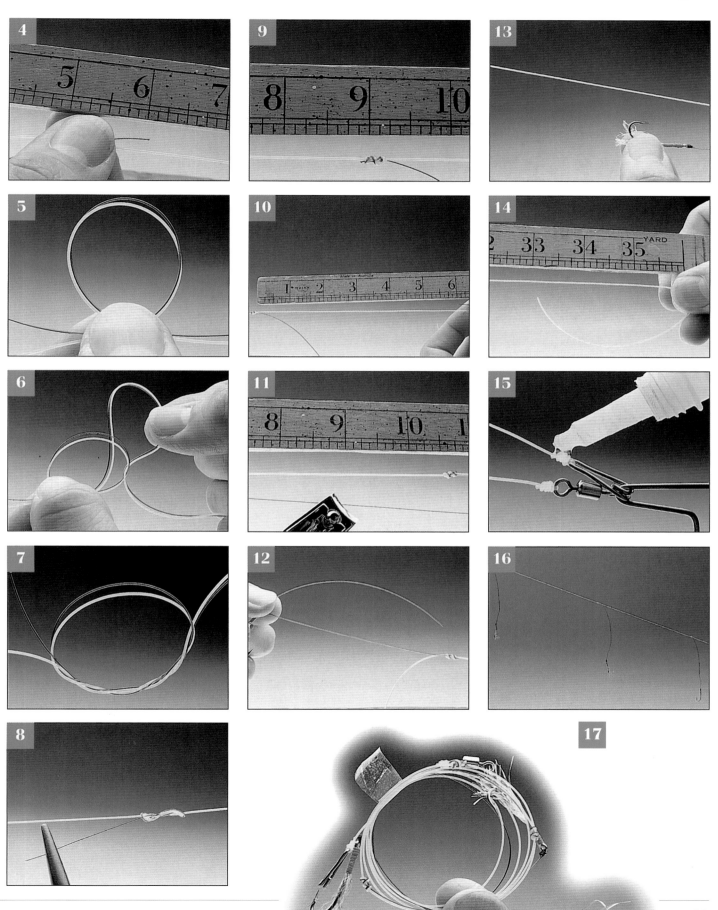

Booms made easy

Follow our simple guide to making your own paternoster boom rigs
which keep the bait fishing away from the main trace

The days of brass wire booms and paternosters have almost slipped into the annals of sea angling history. Without doubt they caught fish, and some will argue that they still do, but there are now many lighter alternatives.

Here we have chosen two plastic/nylon booms that fix to the trace body in completely different ways. The first is the Delta Rotaboom, which is held in place on the trace with Deltabond, a special waterproof glue that does not damage the line.

The other is a conventional plastic boom that has to be trapped between stop knots or crimps.

WHY USE A BOOM?

Booms are popular with anglers hunting flounder, especially when three hooks and crab or harbour ragworm baits are being used.

With a relatively short snood, booms do tend to improve bait presentation, especially if the fish will only take a truly static bait.

The Dab is another type of fish that responds well to booms, so it is always worth keeping a couple of boom rigs in your trace wallet.

ROTABOOM STEP-BY-STEP

1   All you need for a two-hook Delta Rotaboom rig: two booms, two hooks, a swivel, lead link and an optional pair of sequins.
2   Tie the lead link onto the bottom of the 60lb trace body with a Grinner knot.
3   Measure off about 40in of the 60lb line and cut to length. The line is a fairly tight fit in the boom, so trim the end of the trace at an angle with a sharp blade.
4   Thread the two booms on to the trace.
5   Note the longer end faces the lead.

6   Tie the swivel to the head of the trace, which will end up at around 36in.
7   Deltabond, the special adhesive used for securing Rotabooms.
8   The lower boom should be between 10in and 11in above the lead link. With the boom a little above its final position, put a small drop of Deltabond on the line and slide the boom over the glue into place.
9   The second boom should be about 20in or so above the lead link; repeat glue drop and slide into place.
10   The eye of the boom – note the notch where the knot sits.
11   The best type of knot is that old favourite, the Grinner. A simple blood loop will almost certainly slip.
12   Both hook snoods want to be about 10in. Here I have threaded on a single sequin before tying on each hook - size 2 Nordic Bend.
13   Ready for action - the finished trace.

1

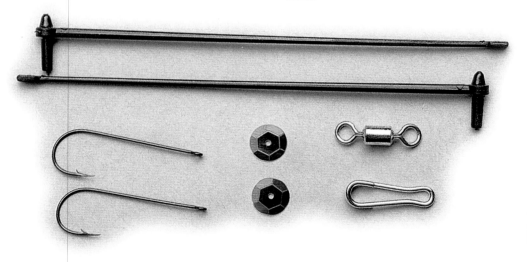

USES OF BOOMS

✔ Popular with anglers who are hunting flounder.
✔ With a relatively short snood they improve bait presentation.
✔ Good for fish that only take a truly static bait.
✔ Keep a couple in your trace wallet.

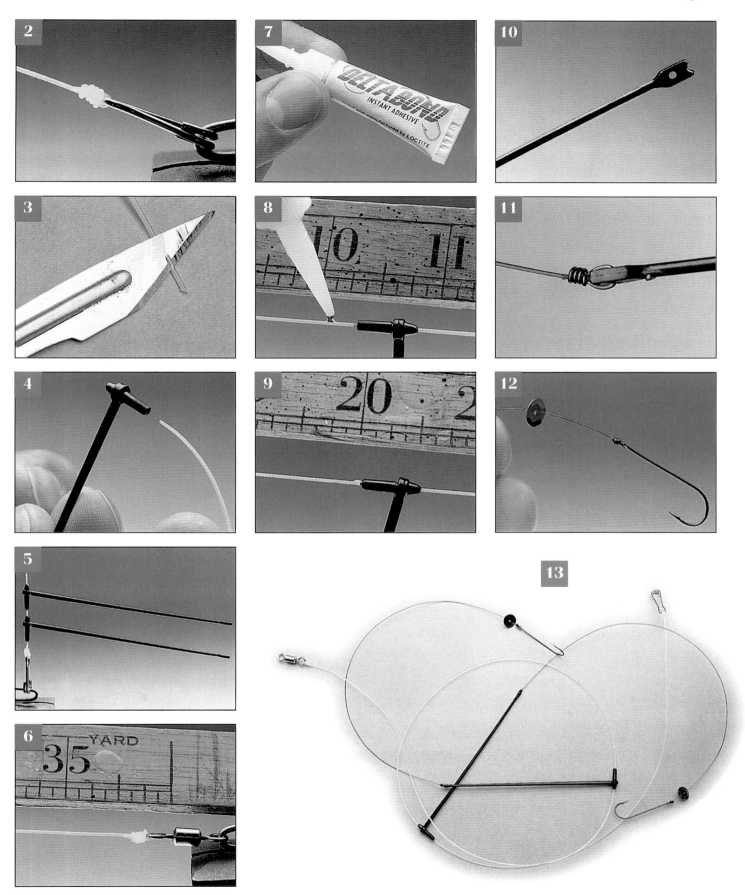

CONVENTIONAL BOOM STEP-BY-STEP

1 You need: two hooks, swivel, lead link plus pair of optional sequins, two booms plus four beads and crimps to hold them.

2 Tie the swivel to the head of the trace body with the trusty Grinner knot.

3 Measure 36in of line. Cut to length.

4 Trim the end of the trace at an angle with a sharp blade to make it easier to thread all the bits and pieces.

5 Thread the booms, beads and crimps on to the trace.

6 Tie lead link on to the end of the trace.

7 Position the lower boom 10in above the lead link, then tighten the crimps. Don't squeeze too hard.

8 With the second boom 10in or so above the lower boom, tighten the crimps.

9 Attach each snood to the boom eye with a Grinner knot.

10 Trim the snood so it is 12in long.

11 One sequin is threaded on each snood before tying on the hook. This often attracts inquisitive fish like flounder and dab.

12 With the hook tied on, snood length is down to 9in or 10in. That shouldn't tangle with anything above or below. With a boom, you can use a much shorter snood than normal, especially if you want the bait to be practically static.

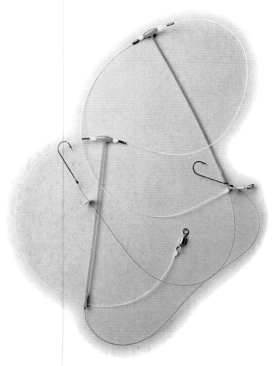

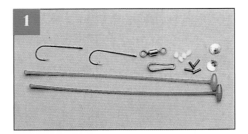

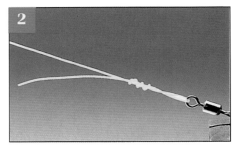

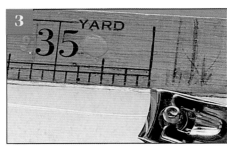

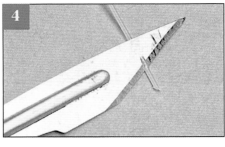

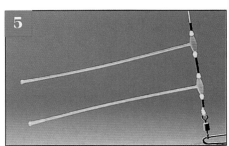

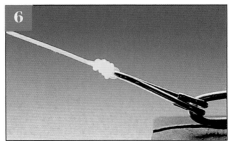

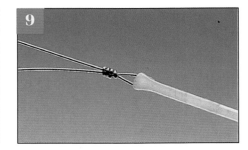

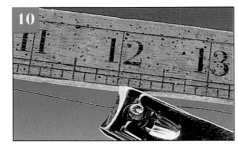

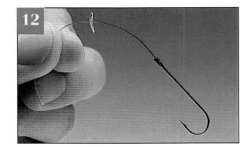

WIN A VIP FISHING TRIP FOR YOU AND EIGHT MATES

www.seaangler.co.uk

SeaAngler

's the biggest, the best and helps make you a better angl

EXCLUSIVE
SPLIT RIG SENSATION

World star, Ian Golds tells us
about his revolutionary rig

TACTICS
PITFALLS OF FISHING STEEP SHINGLE BEACHES SOLVED

THE BEST BEACH COMBOS TESTED

SPORT FISHING
CATCH BIG BASS OFF THE WALL

TOP STORIES
DR WHO
STAR EVE MYLES FIGHTS HOSTILE LIFEFORMS

RED HOT RAY DAY
HOW TO ENJOY SIZZLING THORNBACK ACTION ALONG THE SHORE

What a CATCH!

Sea Angler magazine hits the beaches on the 18th of every month and covers the complete angling scene. It's packed full of expert tips to help make you a better angler.

All the latest methods, rigs and places to catch. It's the magazine that's as important as your bait.

Long-range bomber

The long-range bomber rig is one of the most important developments in terminal tackle over the last decade. Here's how to tie your master blaster!

Few rigs have made such an impact on the match circuit as the bomber rig. It first came to mainstream beach fishing when Essex angler Richard Holgate used the rig to great effect to win the 1992 SAMF Masters final at Southwold in Suffolk.

Just as in the tournament world, where rods are developed and then filter through to beaches, the match circuit is where many top traces see the light of day.

The bomber's main claim to fame is that it will cast two or even three baits a very long way, achieved by having all the baits clipped into a Breakaway Impact Shield, which is positioned immediately behind the lead. Release is practically guaranteed, as long as the trajectory of the cast is not too shallow.

In this bomber example, we have used two single hooks, but a single hook on one snood and a Wishbone or Pennell on the other is often used. With three hooks on one clip however, they need to be fairly small baits.

TOOLS AND COMPONENTS

Main components for assembling this bomber rig are from Dave Docwra's Uni-Trace system, plus a Breakaway Impact Shield. The tools you need are a vice and piece of bent wire, wooden rule, crimping pliers, long-nose pliers, nail clippers and a Stanley knife blade or scalpel.

Trace body is 60lb quality mono, minimum 0.75mm diameter. Hook snoods are 25lb Maxima Chameleon and the stop knots are tied from 0.60mm diameter, 11lb Power Gum.

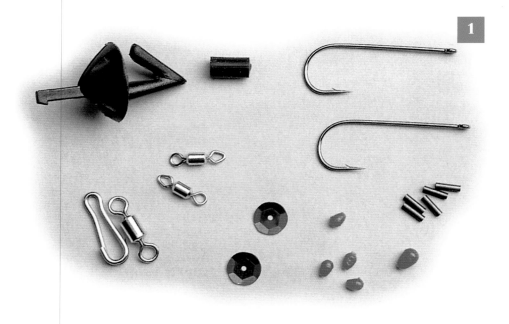

BOMBER RIG STEP-BY STEP

1 The components are: Impact Shield, lead link, top swivel, two snood swivels, beads and crimps. The hooks are size 1 and the sequins also act as bait stops.
2 Tie the top swivel to trace body via a Grinner knot. Cut to length, about 36in.
3 Chamfer the end of the trace with a sharp knife or similar, which will make the beads and crimps much easier to slide on.
4 With all the slide-on components now in place, it's time to tie on the lead link.
5 You can now put a small blob of Superglue on the link and swivel knots for extra security. Apply just one drop of the glue, then carefully wipe off the surplus with a tissue.
6 and 7 The overall trace will be a little over 30in long, with a full length snood and another a little under half that. It is best to tie on the snoods now. You should remember to trim to allow for the hook knot, say about 18in and 34in.
8 Do not tighten the crimps yet.
9 Hold the lower snood swivel 14in above the Impact Shield, and trim snood to just below the lead link.

THE BOMBER RIG

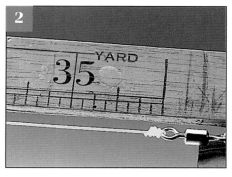

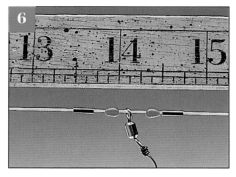

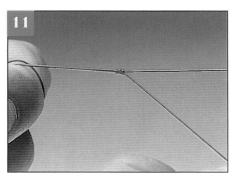

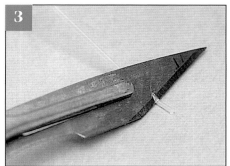

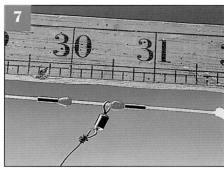

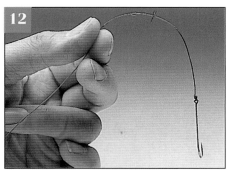

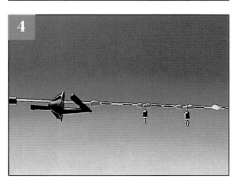

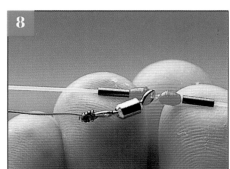

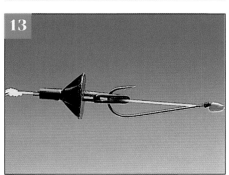

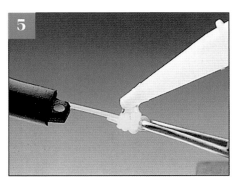

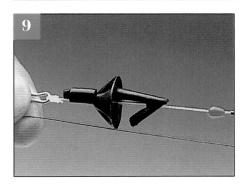

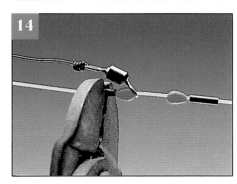

10 Do the same with the top snood, holding it in place 30in above the Shield.
11 With the crimps still not crimped, slide on the sequins and tie on the hooks. Then tie a stop knot 3in or so above the hook with Power Gum.
12 Shows a snood, complete with with hook, sequin and stop knot.

13 Hold the trace body out straight, place lower snood hook in Impact Shield and slide swivel, beads and crimps into place so snood is tight.
14 Now tighten the crimps to fix the swivel firmly in place.

Continued top of next page ▶

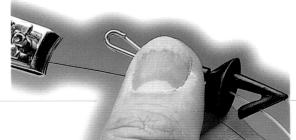

BOMBER RIG *Continued*

15 Repeat steps 14 and 15 to complete the top snood.

16 With both hooks now in place on the Impact Shield, tighten the crimp above so that the bead is just 5mm above the top of the Shield.

17 Here is the completed long-range bomber rig, with sizes and details When you're finished, coil it up neatly, ready to go into that rig wallet for the big fishing trip you always promised yourself.

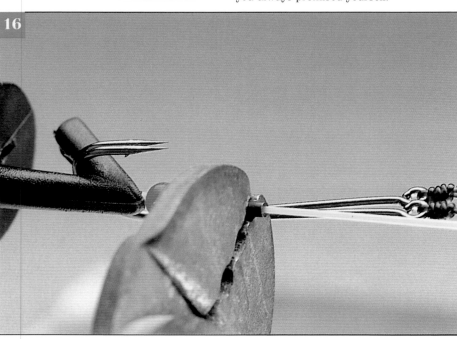

Crimps or stop knots to hold beads

36in 30lb snood

Minimum 12in 30lb snood

Fixed bait clip or Impact Shield

TYING A STOP KNOT

The stop knot is easy enough, but as with most other knots, it's worth practicing a few times to get the knack really covered. Then you're well and truly ready for those moments when you might need to tie one on quickly, when you don't have time to think about it.

A Keep the mainline tight, hold the Powergum next to the mono, with a tag about 4in or 5in long.

B With the Powergum, make four turns around the mainline.

C Now make a loop and make another four turns inside the loop.

D Pull up almost tight, position and finally tighten.

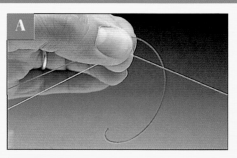

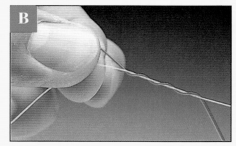

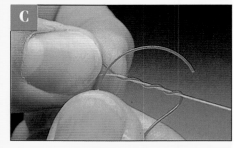

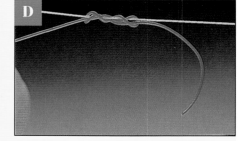

THE ESSENTIAL GRINNER KNOT

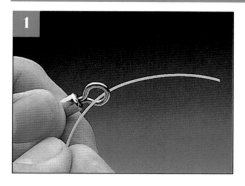

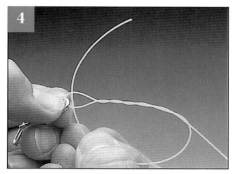

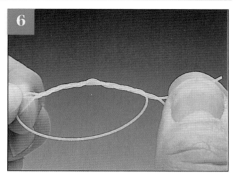

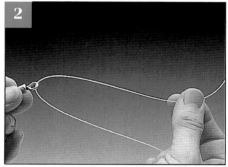

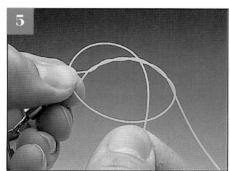

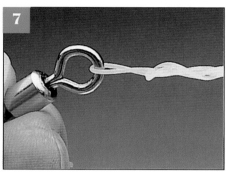

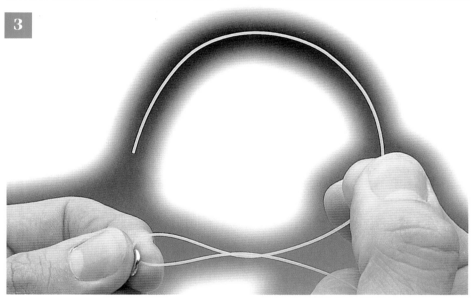

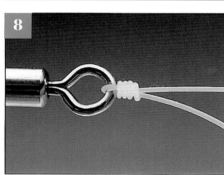

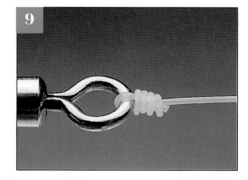

SIMPLE STEP-BY-STEP

1　You can use a Grinner to attach just about anything will a hole in it. First, put the end through the eye.

2　Pull through enough line, so you do not end up with too little line at the end: 6in or so is about right

3　Hold the component and line in one hand, then twist the loose end around the main line.

4　In total, make four turns around the main line, then bring the loose end round in an arc and grip with your left hand to make a loop.

5　Now make a further four turns inside the loop.

6　This results in four turns over a four further turns.

7　Now moisten the whole area with saliva, which helps it all come together. Best done with the swivel held firmly, hold the main line above the knot and slowly pull the loose end.

8　More spit and apply pressure to the main line, moving the knot towards the swivel. Help it on it's way by pulling the knot down the main line if necessary, but if it starts to seize, apply more spit.

9　Having tightened the knot, trim off the loose end as close as you like.

Pulley power

The Pulley rig has been developed by anglers who fish over tackle-snatching rough ground

If you fish over rough ground then you will almost certainly want to fish with a Pulley rig. The object of this type of terminal gear is to prevent the lead hanging down and becoming snagged as you retrieve a hooked fish.

The trace casts like a standard, clipped-down, single snood paternoster, but as soon as you start reeling in with a fish on, the trace retrieves like a running leger.

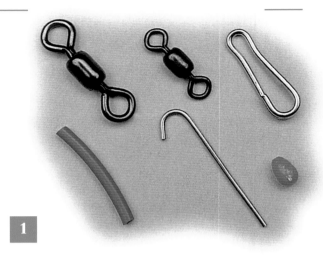

1

PULLEY RIG ESSENTIAL COMPONENTS

This powerful system puts considerable stress on the main body of the trace, where it bends through 180 degrees as it doubles over the main swivel. Therefore line diameter must be stepped up accordingly For this rig we have stepped up the main trace strength from 60lb to 80lb. Along really snaggy parts of the coast some shore anglers go for the safer option and use 90lb line.

It also helps to use a heavier swivel, as the thicker wire helps protect the trace body. Here we use a size 1, 150lb breaking strain, Berkley swivel. Normally used when larger fish are expected, the snood is armed with a sliding Pennell rig, made up with a pair of size 2/0 Viking hooks.

A rotten-bottom is often incorporated into a pulley rig. If you want to fish with this rig turn to page 42, which explains how the rig works and how to tie one up.

PULLEY RIG

SIMPLE STEP-BY-STEP

1 The basic components for our Pulley rig are two swivels (one is the size 1, the other a 65lb breaking strain size 7) bait clip, bead and lead link.

2 Tie the smaller swivel to the trace using a Grinner knot, then slide on the bead, size 1 swivel and the sleeve for the bait clip, before tying on the lead link.

3 The length of the trace body depends on how long a hook snood you will be using. If it's 24in long, once you have tied on the first swivel, cut the trace body to 30in to allow for the link knot.

4 Now is the time to slide in the wire bait clip.

5 Do not forget to round the end of the wire, otherwise it may damage the line or cut through the side of the sleeve.

6 Once you are all the way through, bend the plain end up at right angles to stop it pulling back out.

7 This is a view of the basic trace, before you start tying on the hook snood.

8 Tie on the hook snood, again using a Grinner knot. Then with the lead link in the vice clip, hold the main swivel and pull up tight.

9 Trim the snood to length, allowing a couple of inches for the hook knot.

10 We are using a Pennell rig here, so slide on the top hook, then a small bead and a length of Uni-tube.

11 Now tie on the lower hook.

12 Thread the Uni-tube over the top hook so it sits on the shank of the hook.

13 The finished Pennell; the bead helps stop the hook sliding up and down too easily.

14 With the lead link in the vice wire, hold the main swivel tight so it rests against the stop bead and smaller swivel, then adjust the bait clip.

15 Once everything is in the right place, tie a Power Gum stop knot a couple of millimetres above the bait clip.

16 Tie the large swivel to the end of your leader to use the pulley rig.

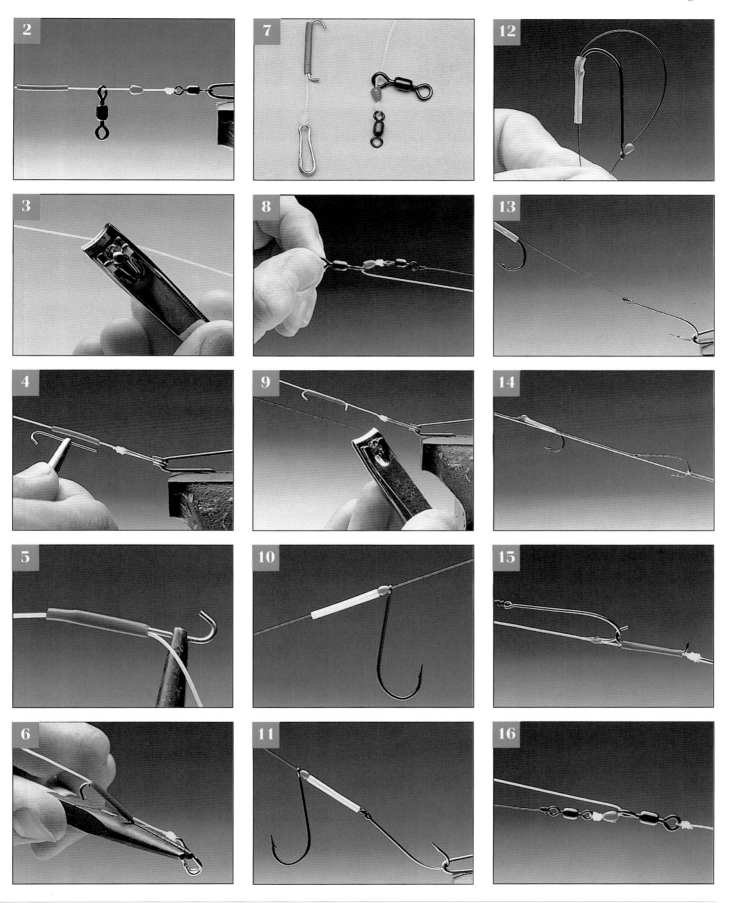

Little rotters

Find out how to cut down on tackle losses by making a rotten-bottom rig for fishing over rocky ground or heavy beds of seaweed

Angling over rough ground can be a nightmare, with heavy tackle losses usually on the cards. But it's not all bad news because there are a few tricks available that can reduce your losses... although you may have to kiss your sinker goodbye! You will need a rotten-bottom to achieve success, and yes, we have heard all the jokes about eating curry, so let's find out why, when and how to use a rotten-bottom.

WHY?

Fishing over rough ground means you face two main problems, both involving the lead weight.

Consider this scenario – once you have cast out and everything has settled, you get a bite, go to pull in and find that the lead is stuck fast. This is even more infuriating when you can feel a good fish thumping away, but are unable to free the lead.

Also, if you hook the fish and are able to free the lead, fine. However, if you cannot get the fish off the bottom quickly and keep it moving, there is a real danger that the lead will snag bottom on the retrieve.

WHEN?

There is little point in using this system over normal ground. Even on moderately lumpy ground a Pulley rig will often get you out of trouble. This is because the weight is pulled up in line with the hook, rather than dangling down, as it would when using a conventional one-hook paternoster.

The time to use a rotten-bottom is when conventional gear gets stuck two casts out of three.

HOW?

A rotten-bottom can be incorporated into most conventional traces. Bait clips can still be used for distance casting, but, with the extra piece of fine line at the base of the trace and the nature of the ground, it's best kept as simple as possible.

ROTTEN BOTTOM CLOSEUP

What goes on beneath the trace is what makes the difference. The idea is that you have a strong connection between the lead and trace for casting, but when it hits the water, these become separated, leaving a weak line that is lighter than your mainline. Should the lead be snagged, a firm pull will either dislodge the lead or break at the weak link. This means you lose the lead, but allows trace and fish to be retrieved as normal.

There are several ways to make a rotten-bottom – here we look at the two most popular. There are variations but they are all basically a loop of line in the end of the trace, used with a float-out pin or clip that holds the lead for the cast, then disengages as soon as it hits the water.

LINE STRENGTH

Line for attaching lead to trace should be lighter than your reel line, so that it snaps before the mainline when pulling for a break. Actual weak link breaking strain will depend on conditions, but if you are using an 18lb mainline, go for a 10lb to 15lb weak link.

If you are too close to your mainline's breaking strain, a damaged mainline section could break before the weak link. If there is a fish on, you should not have to pull so hard for a break that when it goes, the jerk pulls the hook out of the fish.

USING A SHOCKLEADER

Use a shockleader when beach-casting with any of the rigs shown in the book. This acts as a safety device, preventing a lead weight and terminal rig flying off up the beach. The shockleader formula is to multiply the weight of lead in ounces x 10lb shockleader breaking strain. For example: 5oz x 10lb = 50lb leader.

SAFETY FIRST

Take extra care when casting rotten-bottoms. Always use a leader, but remember these methods of temporarily attaching leads are not as strong or reliable as a normal link tied direct to the end of the trace.

Generally, Rotten Bottoms are not suitable for pendulum or power casting or while fishing from crowded piers and breakwaters!

LOOP AND PIN

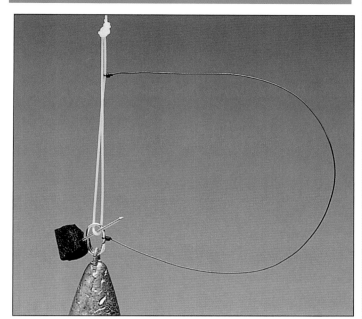

WIRE CLIP

STEP-BY-STEP

A part from your normal trace components, you need an oval link, a short length of light line and a panel pin pushed through a piece of bouyant foam rubber.

◆ Make up your chosen rig as normal, but instead of tying on a lead link, make a loop in the end of the trace.

◆ Tie the length of light line to the loop and the other end to the oval link.

◆ When you want to use it, attach your lead weight to the oval link.

◆ Push the loop in the end of the trace body through the link and insert the pin into the protruding loop.

◆ Pull the loop back until the pin is resting on the oval, preventing the loop pulling through.

◆ The action of the lead hitting the water is often enough to dislodge the pin. If not, as soon as it hits the bottom and tension is relieved, the foam will simply float away, drawing the pin out of the loop.

STEP-BY-STEP

There are various clips that enable near normal casting, although you might have to look around in order to find a shop that sells them. Once you have one the step-by step is easy.

◆ Simply tie the clip to the end of your trace in place of the normal link. The sinker loops sits in the open bend of the hook, as shown.

◆ Tie a length of light line to the clip link eye and attach the other end of the mono to the oval link or directly to the sinker loop.

◆ Hang the lead on the open end of the clip and cast, making sure you give it a bit of slack line as the trace hits the water, to help the sinker slip free.

THE ROTTEN BOTTOM IN ACTION

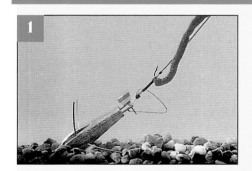

1 Here the lead has landed on the sea bed and the bouyant release pin is still held in place.

2 The pin begins to float free as the tension on the main trace goes slack.

3 Up floats the pin releasing the trace. Now the heavier trace is linked to the sinker by the lighter length of line.

Tales of the unexpected

Why visit the same old angling spots when a change of scenery can rekindle the interest in your fishing? Alan Yates explains why the challenge of a new venue should be greeted with excitement, not fear and despair!

I t's always an attractive challenge to fish a new venue for the very first time. There's so much to learn from all those contributing factors which you hope will combine to help you actually catch something that's well worthwhile.

There's no doubt that familiarity with a certain fishing spot breeds contempt, as the angler learns which state of tide is best, that peeler crab is the top bait and daylight hours are useless, for example.

Those basic rules about each venue become engraved in our memory simply because the facts and features of success and failure are remembered, so they can be repeated or avoided.

But it usually takes a first time visitor or a novice angler to remind you that fishing is never completely cut and dried,

◄ One that came out of the blue and didn't get away.

or that a well-known venue is not without its surprises.

Several years ago, I remember taking a friend to a cod mark I had fished as both man and boy. He promptly hooked and landed one of the biggest shore bass I had ever seen from 'my spot'! Was it sheer chance or had I overlooked something about the venue?

The answer was that for years I had overcast the bass and was intent on casting long for the cod. Since that big bass, I have caught several others from my spot, but none as big.

There are two basic approaches to fishing a new venue. Firstly, the angler

▲ Always expect the unexpected. Gerry with his surprise 12lb 8oz bass.
► Matchman Gerry Byrne carries his trophy bass triumphantly up the beach.

must obtain as much information about the fishing as they can. The local tackle dealer, other anglers, catch guides, coastal reports, books and videos all offer valuable information, which without, much is left to chance, imagination and logic.

The bonus side of the instinctive approach is that you're unbiased by factual information, and some would say, it's more enjoyable than taking everything for granted. However, few anglers would deliberately set out to fish a new venue without any inside info. This is left to the more experienced angler, who is less likely to proceed by trial and error.

Continued on page 44 ►

42

For some, fishing a new venue is addictive, they must progress from place to place, proving or disproving each and every pier, beach or estuary.

New venues are a challenge. The 'straightjacket' of pre-conceived opinion through fishing the same spot, on the same pier, year in, year out, is definitely not for them.

But for the rest of us, fishing a new venue is an occasional and often exciting bonus. Just a change in the scenery can be a shot in the arm, while the prospect of a different species or bigger fish can whet the appetite.

EXPLORE THE EMERALD ISLE

Ireland is one place where fishing can still surprise and there's always the chance of a specimen when you least expect it. On a recent journey to Clare in Western Ireland, I paused in Dublin to collect bait and have a couple of days fishing with members of the Irish Match and Surfcasting Association, IMASA.

Dublin tackle dealer, Mick Dixon, who I have known for many years, offered to take myself and companion, John Wells, to a new venue in search of thornback ray. Mick's chosen venue, because of a strong north-easterly wind, was Ennereilly Strand which is sheltered behind Mixxen Head to the south of Dublin.

IMASA match records reveal that in the same week in 1991, no less than 35 ray came from the venue during a five-hour match. An hour's drive on the Wexford road, south of Wicklow and we came to Britas Bay, where we parked up in a small cliff top car park.

Below, and 80 yards out from a deserted sandy beach, a line of white surf

Another day, a new venue and a fresh challenge for matchman Pete Owen.

broke in a straight line to disturb a hidden sand bar. The gulls circled gaps in the surf, which gave away the deep holes, occasionally diving... the complete scene screamed fish and I couldn't load up my tackle and get down the cliff quick enough.

My match angling logic suggested I should walk as far up the beach as I needed, to get on the end of the line of anglers. John Wells joined me and we took the end peg uptide of a brown patch, alongside a defined deep hole or gap in the sand bar. The most obvious tactic to catch a ray was to cast a sand eel or peeler crab into the deeper patches of brown water on the down slopes of the bar.

A single hook rig with long snood and plain lead (we didn't want to scare the ray) with grip wires was set up in haste. While

the frozen sand eel were thawing from the food flask, Mick told us that the odd bass was caught from the gully inside the sand bar. A second rod was set up and a 3/0 Cox and Rawle uptide hook was baited with a large cocktail of peeler and mackerel – locally called a Wicklow special – and cast 70 yards. As we tackled up, two more anglers moved up the beach past us, and I remarked to John that our end peg advantage had gone. Almost immediately after the pair had cast, a bass took one of their baits, which was aimed at a ray, and Dublin matchman Gerry Byrne had a fight on his hands.

The fish surfaced, as is typical of bass, and fought hard all the way to the beach where it was dragged from the surf, bending the 3/0 long shank Kamasan Aberdeen almost straight!

RIG SHOPPING LIST

The fishing went well with the following items:
- ◆ 36in snood ◆ Snood swivel
- ◆ Trace swivel ◆ Two beads
- ◆ Two crimps ◆ Link
- ◆ 150gr sinker
- ◆ 79515 3/0 Viking

Fishing stopped as we gathered around to admire the fish, which was perhaps the biggest beach bass I had ever seen. At 80cm long it should have shattered the Irish record, but its lean body and empty stomach meant that when it was weighed, it scaled just 12lb 8oz!

We never did catch a ray and added only a few dogfish, but the bass made the trip and I must admit drained me of motivation the minute it was landed. It was a fish of a lifetime... even for a spectator.

LEARN FROM YOUR CATCHES

The whole episode certainly proved that experience, plus a small grain of local information, can prove to be absolutely invaluable to success and is an example of how bass can turn up out of the blue or

when conditions are really not ideal.

Their liking of surf and close proximity to the shoreline have produced lots of other examples of surprise catches and this possibly gives us an important clue as to where to go bass fishing.

However, how many experienced anglers are happy to spend time plopping in the surf in search of a giant bass, especially when there are dab, whiting and other species to provide action on almost every cast?

The best tactics you can use to cover

▲ *What a specimen!*

both options in such situations are to use two rods, one to them to build a bag of 'bits' at range and the other to fish short with a big bait.

The trouble is that when the bass does strike, it always takes a hook aimed at something else and is not often seen, let alone landed! Just remember that in angling, even getting it wrong can be the best way to find success...

Set the standard

The standard running rig is probably the most widely used terminal outfit in the boat angler's armoury

Fished with the right bait, the standard running rig will take most fish swimming in British waters.

Here we show you how to build a standard running leger for uptiding. Such a running leger is easily the most efficient and productive method if you like uptiding for cod, bass, smoothhound and ray.

Key factors to consider when tying up this type of rig are the strength of tide, type of bait and primary target species. The whole object of uptiding is to ensure that your bait fishes hard on the sea bed, because when fishing in a very strong run of tide, the flow of water can easily lift the bait off the bottom.

For the reason above it is highly advisable to use relatively short hooklengths, in the region of 3ft to 4ft long in very strong tides, progressively increasing the length as the tide eases off.

GETTING READY

twin-hook Pennell rig will invariably help to increase the overall bait presentation when using baits such as worm or squid. It also provides additional hooking power with a hook at either end of a large bait.

Many anglers tie their hooklengths from line which is far too light in breaking strain and unreliable. You should almost always use 50lb mono for uptide hooklengths.

Grip leads are usually used for uptiding in order to keep the terminal rig nailed hard on the bottom. There will always be a possibility of the hooklength tangling around the wires during casting. The likelihood of this happening can be greatly reduced by using a tubi-type sliding boom to attach the lead. One with an overall length of around 4in should be sufficient.

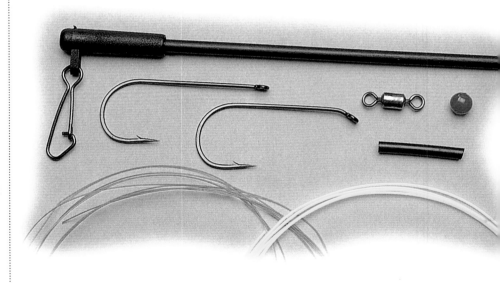

SIMPLE STEP-BY-STEP

1 The basic components for the rig are: Plastic boom, 100lb Berkley-type swivel, two beads, two Mustad Viking hooks, rubber tube for the Pennell hook and two different coloured lines to distinguish mainline (yellow) from snood line (red).

Rolling swivel

Small bead stops sliding boom jamming on leader knot

4in boom

Bead

4ft, 50lb breaking strain hooklength

RUNNING LEGER

Pennell rig using size 2/0-6/0 Uptide Viking hooks

Breakout lead weight

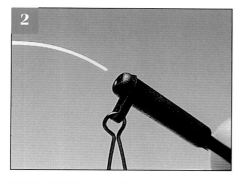

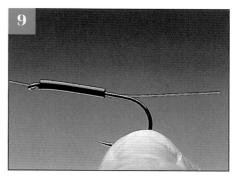

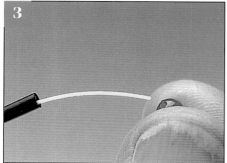

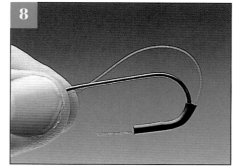

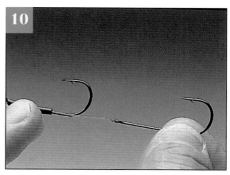

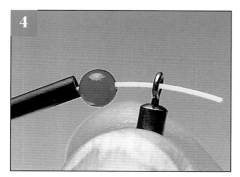

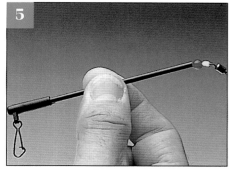

STEP-BY-STEP *Continued*

2   Slide the boom over the mainline with the lead link furthest from the hook.

3   Pull through, then slide bead on to mainline. The bead stops the boom end slamming into the knot during casting or while playing a weighty fish.

4   Now tie the swivel on to the end of the mainline.

5   This is what it should look like prior to the hooklength being attached.

6   Close-up detail of the boom end, showing the bead protecting the knot and the snood length attached to the other side of the swivel.

7   The traditional 79510 Viking with a turned-in eye is threaded on the snood, followed by a length of rubber tube

8   Once threaded on the snood line, slide the rubber tube over hook point and around the bend.

9   This is how the rubber tube should end up on the shank.

10   Now tie on the bottom hook, a 79515 Viking with a straight eye, to form the Pennell.

11   The finished article, complete with a breakout lead for uptiding.

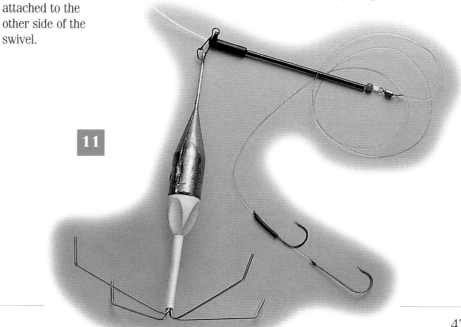

Flattie fantastic

Bet there are not many anglers who think of tying a flashing spoon into the end of their boat rig. Well, it's a thing you have got to learn to do if you want to catch a flatfish!

Many anglers have a tendency to over-complicate a spoon rig intended for fishing on the drift for flatfish. However, the very nature of the rig and drifting techniques mean that this is certainly one outfit that can tangle in a flash. The spooning rig shown here is about as simple as you can get and is by far the most efficient. Note that the overall length is very long, compared to other boat rigs. This extra length gives a more natural presentation over sand, where it works best. To minimise any risk of the long hooklength tangling around the mainline during its descent to the bottom, there are two important factors to note.

GETTING READY

The first factor to consider is the use of a long tube-type boom, which effectively helps to keep the hooklength well away from the mainline.

The second factor is that this rig should always be lowered to the bottom slowly. Knock the reel into free spool, hold on to the weight and drop the baited hook and spoon into the water.

Allow the tide and drift of the boat to fully straighten the hooklength before releasing the lead and allowing the rig to fall steadily to the bottom.

This rig is intended for the likes of plaice and dab, but larger fish such as turbot and ray are often caught over the same marks.

When there is a possibility of hooking a bonus fish you should upgrade the standard long-shanked, fine-wire Aberdeen hook for a Mustad Viking No 79515, usually between size 1 and 1/0.

The extra strength of wire improves the chances of landing any large fish, though this is not a technique that is generally used over rough ground.

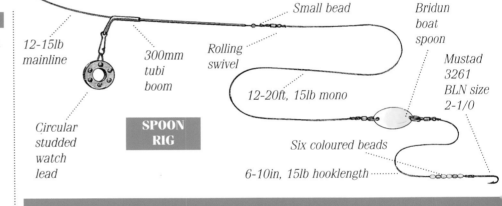

SPOON RIG

- 12-15lb mainline
- Circular studded watch lead
- 300mm tubi boom
- Rolling swivel
- Small bead
- 12-20ft, 15lb mono
- Six coloured beads
- 6-10in, 15lb hooklength
- Bridun boat spoon
- Mustad 3261 BLN size 2-1/0

1

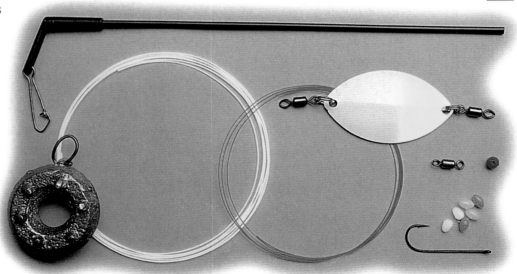

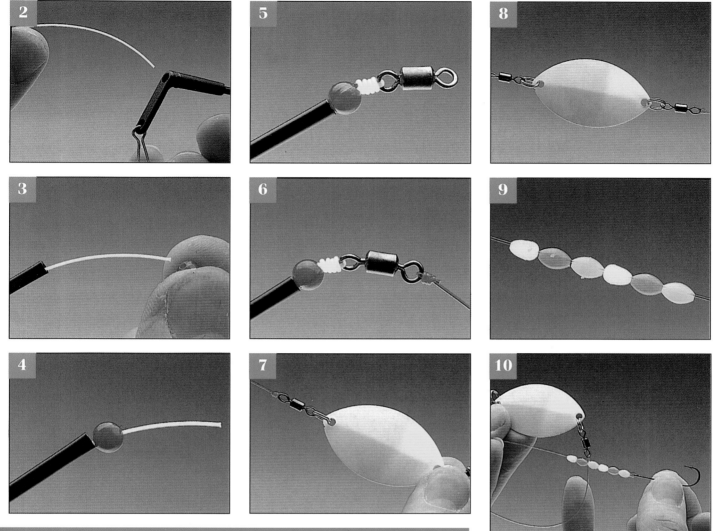

SPOON RIG STEP-BY-STEP

1 Items that you need: boom, attractor beads, 100lb Berkley-type swivel, Aberdeen hook, spoon and line, red for the snood and yellow representing mainline.

2 When inserting mainline into the boom, keep the lead link end of boom furthest from the hook.

3 Pull line through, then slide bead onto mainline.

4 The bead in place.

5 The swivel has now been tied on.

6 Now tie the snood line to the other end of the swivel.

7 Tie boat spoon to end of snood line.

8 Another length of snood line has been attached to the opposite end of the spoon.

9 Slide on half a dozen attractor beads.

10 Tie the hook to the end of the snood

11 The completed flatfish rig with spoon tied 6 to 10 inches above the hook

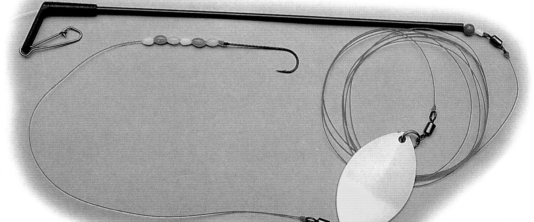

Get the drift

To present an artificial sandeel so that it looks like the real thing means you have to fish it off a very finally balanced long flowing trace. Here's how to make one.

Fishing on the drift with an artificial sandeel is one of the most productive and popular techniques – it's used by anglers to catch pollack, coalfish, bass and cod over wrecks and reefs.

The single most important factor affecting your success when using this rig is that the artificial eel must be allowed to swim in a lifelike and attractive manner. To achieve this the eel is fished off a long hooklength.

You should use a long tubi-type boom, too. This is an item that definitely minimises the very real risk you can run of the hooklength tangling around the mainline during its descent to the bottom.

GETTING READY

With the reel in free-spool the eel is released over the side of the boat, allowing the drift of the boat to fully straighten the hooklength out. Only then is the lead weight released, and allowed to fall steadily to the bottom.

It is always best to use bomb-shaped leads which will fall smoothly through the water. Flat bottomed or circular leads have a tendency to twist and turn causing tangles during the descent.

A small swivel tied approximately half way along the hooklength can also help reduce twisting, if the artificial eel starts to spin. There must be a fair run of tide or wind to push the boat along on a good speed of drift for this method to work effectively. It is generally ineffective around slack water.

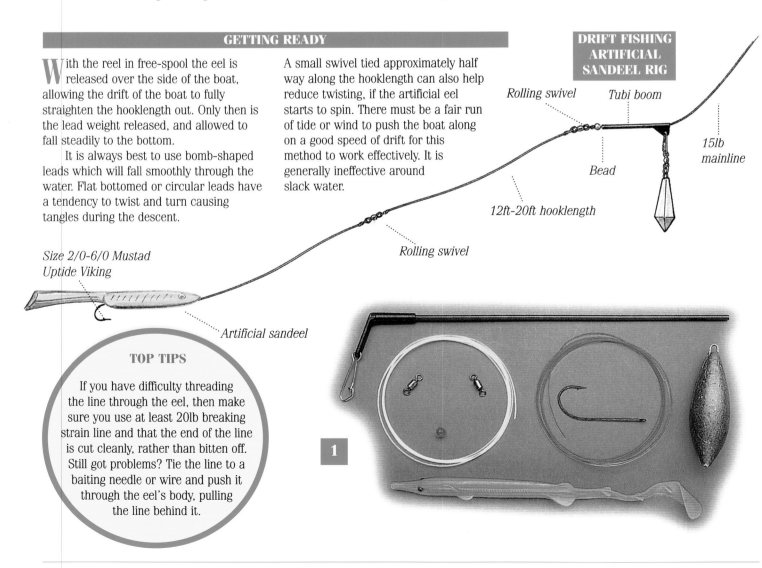

DRIFT FISHING ARTIFICIAL SANDEEL RIG

Rolling swivel

Tubi boom

Bead

15lb mainline

12ft-20ft hooklength

Rolling swivel

Size 2/0-6/0 Mustad Uptide Viking

Artificial sandeel

TOP TIPS

If you have difficulty threading the line through the eel, then make sure you use at least 20lb breaking strain line and that the end of the line is cut cleanly, rather than bitten off. Still got problems? Tie the line to a baiting needle or wire and push it through the eel's body, pulling the line behind it.

1

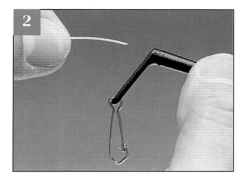

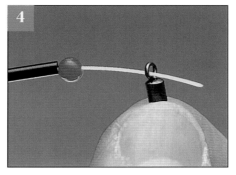

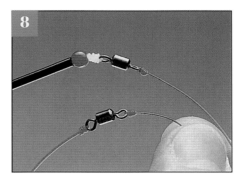

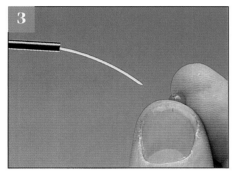

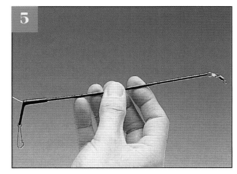

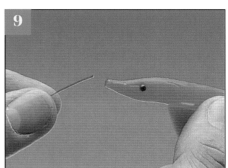

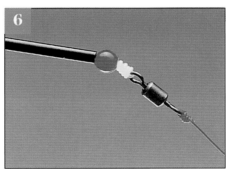

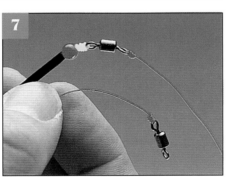

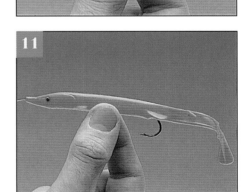

STEP-BY-STEP

1 The picture at bottom left shows the items that you need: boom, lead, a couple of 100lb Berkley swivels, bead, main and snood line, plus of course, the artificial eel.

2 Slide the end of the mainline into the lead link end of the boom.

3 Pull the line through and slide on the bead that will protect the knot from the end of the boom.

4 Now add the first swivel.

5 Now carefully attach, using a standard grinner knot

6 Tie the first length of trace line to the swivel.

7 Now tie the second swivel on to the first trace length.

8 Here is the second snood, attached to the second swivel.

9 Gently remove the hook, and now thread the end of the trace into the mouth of the eel.

10 The line should come out of the vent.

11 Tie the hook, and pull the hook shank back into the body of the eel.

12 This picture shows the complete rig. The second swivel will help control some of the line twist created by the eel as it moves about in the tide.

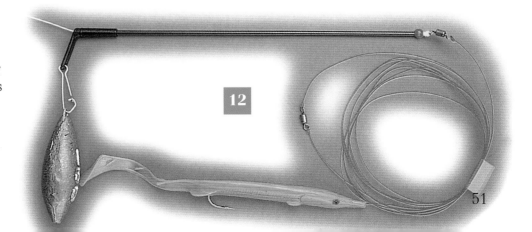

Watch those teeth

These pages concentrate on a rig for dealing with fish that have teeth, like tope, reef conger and spurdog. Based on a standard running trace, the rig terminates in a heavy biting or rolling trace

The primary consideration when fishing for tope, conger and spurdog is their sharp teeth and strong jaws. These make short work of standard mono, so you have to use either a wire hooklength or heavy-duty mono to prevent fish biting through.

Use heavy mono, that's line between 150lb and 250lb, for tope or conger fishing. However, when general fishing use wire because it offers better bait presentation and is far more supple than thick mono.

Another consideration is the use of a length of reasonably heavy line, usually mono of around 50lb, to act as a rubbing length between the actual hooklength and the mainline.

This is especially important when targeting tope, which have a rough skin and an annoying tendency to roll up the mainline and break thinner lines. A standard shockleader of around 20ft in length is ideal for solving this problem.

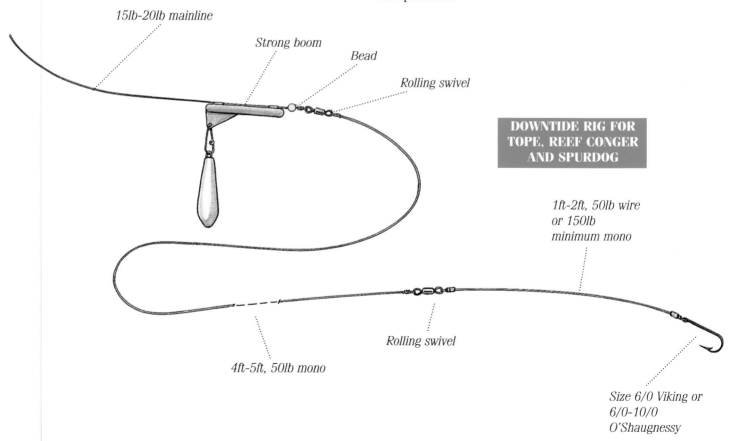

15lb-20lb mainline

Strong boom

Bead

Rolling swivel

DOWNTIDE RIG FOR TOPE, REEF CONGER AND SPURDOG

1ft-2ft, 50lb wire or 150lb minimum mono

Rolling swivel

4ft-5ft, 50lb mono

Size 6/0 Viking or 6/0-10/0 O'Shaugnessy

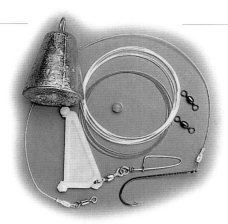

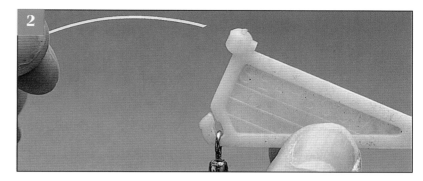

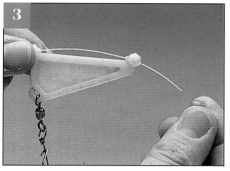

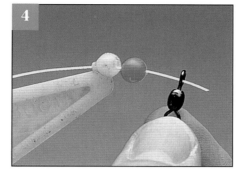

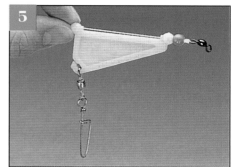

SIMPLE STEP-BY-STEP

1 The components that you need on display – boom, bead, 100lb Berkley-type swivel, 50lb wire trace or 50lb mono headed by a size 6/0 Viking or size 6/0 to 10/0 O'Shaughnessy hook, plus snood line (red) and mainline, (yellow)

2 First, slide the boom on to the mainline, with the lead link on the boom furthest from the hook

3 Pull the line through and then thread on a bead.

4 Tie on the swivel, making quite sure that the knot is snugged right down and really tight.

5 Here the boom is shown assembled. Note the bead protecting the knot to the swivel.

6 Here the snood line has been tied to the swivel.

7 And shown in this picture, the wire trace has now been tied to the other end of the snood

8 Here you can see the completed trace, complete with the bell shaped lead which is ideal for holding a big fish bait, securely on the sea bed.

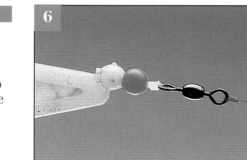

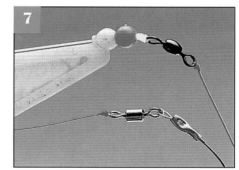

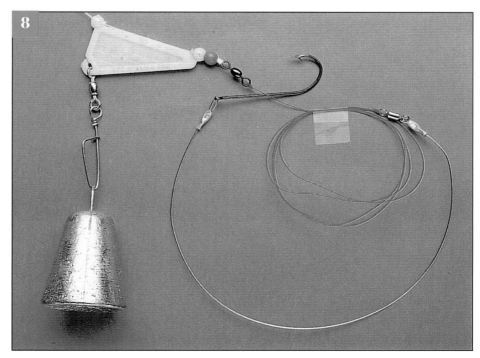

Small wonder

The trick for fishing the right terminal rig is getting the balance right so the bait fishes naturally on the bottom. This rig is designed for fishing small baits when catch rates are slowing down

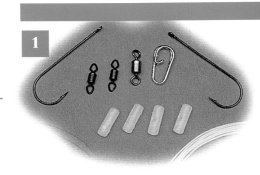

This rig is effectively the same as the sort of paternoster rig often used by shore anglers. Boat anglers use either two or three snoods off the main rig body.

It is an ideal rig to use afloat when you wish to experiment with a selection of different baits or when you are trying to catch as many fish as possible, like in a competition.

There are many methods which can be used to attach the individual hooklengths, ranging from swivels trapped between two beads, to paternoster booms. Swivels are not only cheap, but help to tie an extremely effective no-nonsense and tangle-free terminal rig.

This type of rig can be used more or less anywhere, over rough and clean ground, both at anchor and on the drift.

Obviously, hook sizes can be changed to accommodate different size baits and target species, although this rig type is often associated with smaller species.

The backbone of the trace should be tied from a minimum of 50lb mono and the hooklengths between 25lb and 50lb, depending on target species.

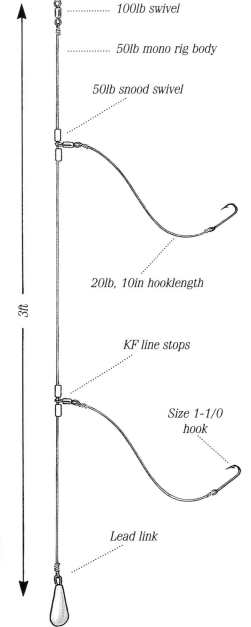

- 100lb swivel
- 50lb mono rig body
- 50lb snood swivel
- 20lb, 10in hooklength
- KF line stops
- Size 1-1/0 hook
- Lead link

3ft

SCRATCHING RIG

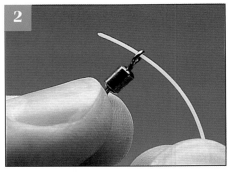

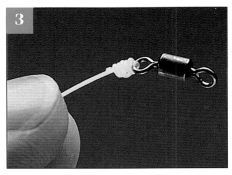

SIMPLE STEP-BY-STEP

1 Here is the equipment that you need: 100lb Berkley-type swivel, two 50lb Berkley-type snood swivels, an Easy Link, four KF line stops and a couple of hooks; plus snood line (shown red) and mainline (shown yellow).
2 Thread the end of the main body line through the eye of the main swivel.
3 Tie on the swivel using a grinner knot.
4 Lay out the stops and swivels in the order they are to be put on to the trace.
5 Slide on the first stop.
6 Now the swivel.
7 Then the second stop.
8 This is the sort of gap to leave between the two stops with the swivel trapped in between.
9 Now all the stops and swivels have been mounted in the trace, check they are in the right order.

SCRATCHING RIG

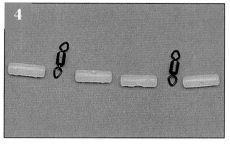

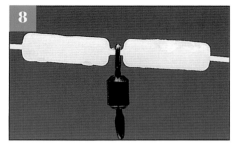

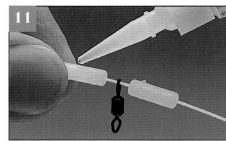

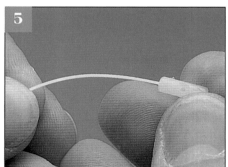

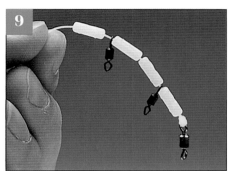

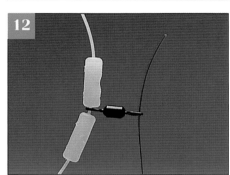

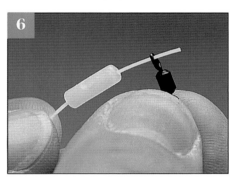

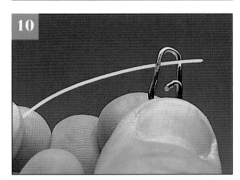

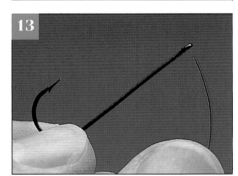

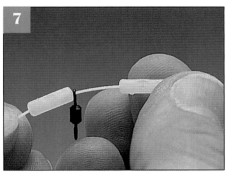

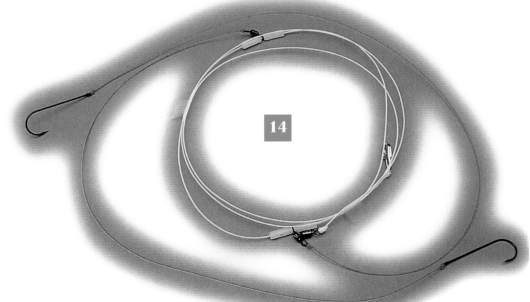

10 Tie on the Easy Link which is used to attach the sinker.

11 With the stops and swivel in place, place a drop of Superglue in the cavity to fix them in place. Warning – DON'T get this glue on your fingers: you've a good chance of being permanently attached if you do.

12 Now tie on the hook snoods...

13 ... and finally the hooks.

14 The finished paternoster rig.

Seen it, caught it

Ask a boat angler what his favourite boat rig is and he is bound to answer, a downtide running rig with a flyer above the lead. If you don't know how to tie one up, then now is the time to learn!

This must rate as the most commonly used of all of the boat rigs – you could say it has seen most fish, caught them and got the tee-shirt.

There's not too much you can say about a simple downtide running leger rig, except that much of its effectiveness lies in its simplicity.

You can either use purpose-made lead carrying booms, as shown in the diagram, or a simple cheap American snap link when fishing over very rough ground and tackle losses are likely to be high.

Never be tempted to compromise on quality when choosing a swivel to join the hooklength to the mainline. Even a relatively small fish is more than capable of exerting a heavy pressure on the trace, especially when you are pumping the fish

back towards the boat against the tide. Low-quality swivels will snap.

The overall length of the hooklength is important. Use a short hooklength when fishing in very fast tides, which will help to keep the bait on the sea bed.

When fishing in lighter tides a longer hooklength will offer a more natural bait presentation.

Hook sizes should be chosen to suit the size of your baits and the target species. Tackle losses can be kept at a minimum when fishing over very rough ground by attaching the lead with a short length of light mono or sandwich bag tie which will easily snap under load.

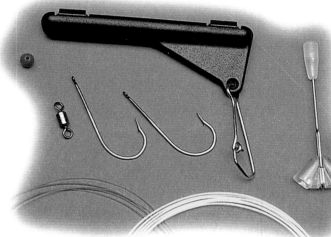

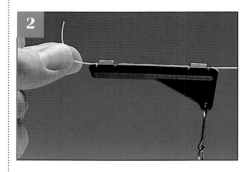

1 You need: 100lb swivel, bead, boom for weight, paternoster boom or three-way swivel (they are cheaper), a pair of hooks and some line, here shown red for snoods, yellow for mainline
2 Slide the lead boom on the mainline...
3 ... and follow with a bead.
4 Then attach the swivel.
5 Tie the bottom trace to the swivel...
6 ... so that it looks like this.

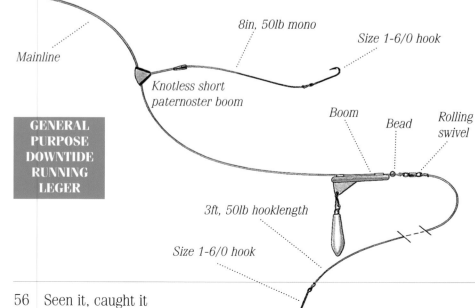

Mainline

8in, 50lb mono

Size 1-6/0 hook

Knotless short paternoster boom

GENERAL PURPOSE DOWNTIDE RUNNING LEGER

Boom

Bead

Rolling swivel

3ft, 50lb hooklength

Size 1-6/0 hook

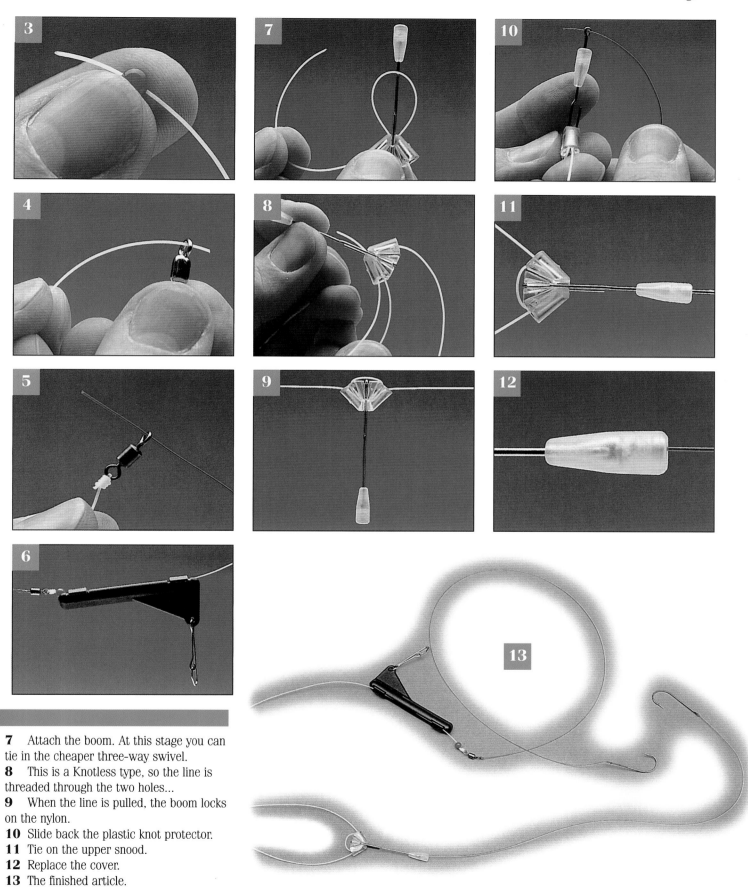

7 Attach the boom. At this stage you can tie in the cheaper three-way swivel.
8 This is a Knotless type, so the line is threaded through the two holes...
9 When the line is pulled, the boom locks on the nylon.
10 Slide back the plastic knot protector.
11 Tie on the upper snood.
12 Replace the cover.
13 The finished article.

Deadly drifter

Basic in the extreme, heavy and deadly. That's the best way of describing the multi-hook rigs used by wreck anglers to catch cod, pollack, coalfish and even ling... if you bait the hook!

This particular rig may not be a great favourite with sporting anglers who prefer to catch fish on an individual basis. However, the combination of a pirk and a string of muppets, feathers or other lures working together can be used with deadly effect. Typically this type of rig will be used by anglers fishing for the likes of cod, ling, pollack and coalfish, either over wrecks or reefs.

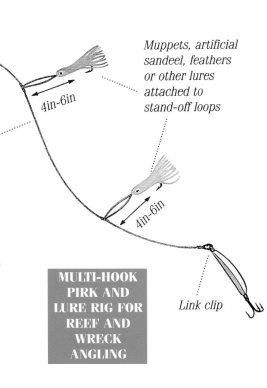

Rolling swivel

Main line

Muppets, artificial sandeel, feathers or other lures attached to stand-off loops

4in-6in

60lb main line

4in-6in

MULTI-HOOK PIRK AND LURE RIG FOR REEF AND WRECK ANGLING

Link clip

Due to the ever present, indeed likely, risk of multiple hook-ups, it is very important that the backbone of the trace is tied from very strong quality mono.

When fishing over rough ground the standard treble hook attached to the pirk weight can be swapped for a single hook, which greatly reduces the risk of the pirk snagging.

This is also worth doing when you wish to use bait to boost the attraction of your lures, notably when fishing for ling. It is far easier to mount baits efficiently on to a single hook rather than a treble.

This type of rig is almost always used when fishing on the drift. It is very important the trace fishes in as near a vertical line as possible for it to work at its maximum efficiency. This not only helps to reduce the risk of snagging, but greatly boosts the number of fish caught.

It will usually be necessary to change the size of pirk used several times throughout the state of one tide to help maintain a vertical line. The stronger the tide, the heavier the lead.

MULTI-HOOK RIG STEP-BY-STEP

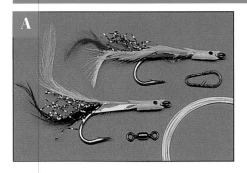

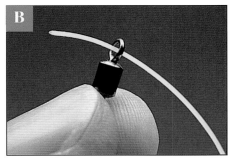

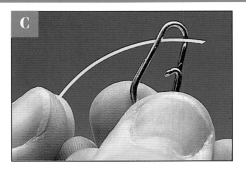

A   Here are the components that you need: muppets, artificial eels, feathers, top swivel, link and heavy-duty mono trace.

B   First of all, carefully tie the swivel to one end of the trace. This is rather fiddly work, but the end results make it a worthwhile exercise.

C   With the swivel tied firmly, now you can go on and tie the link to the other end.

MAKING A BLOOD LOOP

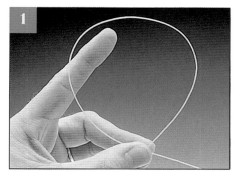

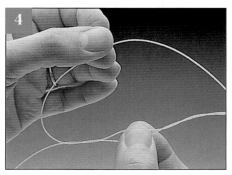

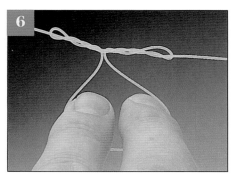

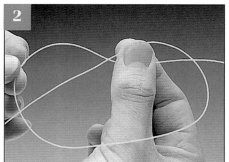

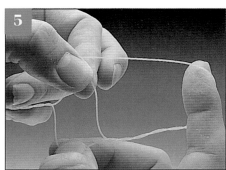

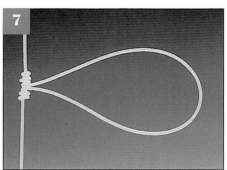

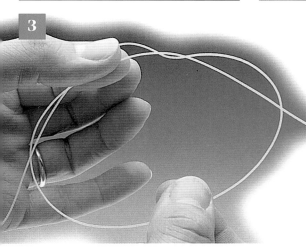

SIMPLE STEP-BY-STEP

1 Twist the line into a full loop, keeping the loop large enough to get your finger through.

2 Turn the loop into a lop-sided figure eight. It helps if you keep one end anchored.

3 Now grip the smaller left-hand loop with your left hand, then swing the large loop all the way round and back to where you started. You will have to release the left hand, but make sure that you keep the small loop in place.

4 This is what it should look like after three complete turns.

5 Here's where an extra hand would be useful, just to make things a bit easier! Hold the main loop steady, then carefully tease out the smaller loop that you have been holding.

6 Pull most of the loop through, until the outer coils start to come together.

7 The completed blood loop, tied and tightened.

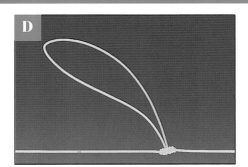

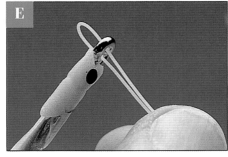

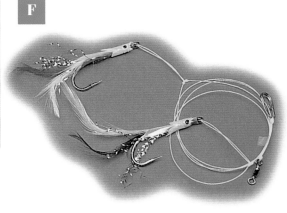

D Tie two blood loops in the trace.

E Attach the lures by threading the loop through hook eye and over the hook shank, pulling tight so they stand off the trace.

F Here you can see the finished trace, less pirk. You can use a lead or even a tie in a weak rotten-bottom if you are fishing over rough ground.

Have we got news for you!

Pack your pirks and grease those gears as we motor to a distant southern North Sea mark in search of some rod-wrenching cod

Next time some bar fly collars you in the boozer and tells you there are no cod in the North Sea, stare him straight in the eye and reply, in a knowing sort of way, rowlocks! Follow us now to a series of wrecks which will have you hurrying to the nearest charter boat, anxious to get your rod loaded! John McKenzie reports...

▼ *Editor Mel Russ found a string of white feathers pulled the cod.*

We're about to prove there are still cod, and good numbers of them, to be caught, the places you should be trying and the skipper who will make sure you get your rod pulled.

But surely you're never guaranteed brilliant fishing, or are you? Will the skipper's knowledge, access to good marks and the willingness of the anglers, all mix to make a recipe for success?

We thought it was time to put the ingredients to the test and booked a trip off Ramsgate in Kent aboard Dave Barrett's boat, *Que Sera Sera*.

Although Ramsgate isn't one of the 'fashion' ports for wreck fishing, it is an area with a wealth of history, heaps of wrecks and endless offshore sport.

Cod, pollack, bass and conger – the chance is there and Dave's background also makes a trip that much more confidence building. He was a commercial skipper for over 20 years and with a 'little black book' full of wrecks to try, he can put you on fish like no other man.

Dave is definitely 'the man' with technology at his fingertips and we thought it was time to muscle in on his beamy 33ft catamaran to find out the true story.

Moving to the target

As Dave moved the cursor on the screen of his electronic navigation system to a noted wreck, we carried on steaming away into the distance, leaving the bustling port behind and heading for the 'dot' on the horizon. Our target was about 34 miles offshore, a tiny, thin wreck which had proved fruitful for Dave and countless charter customers in the past.

Dave commented: "It's not the bigger the wreck, the bigger the catch. I've caught a lot of cod from wrecks which have been virtually covered in sand. It's weird the way some places attract more fish than others, I don't know why that is. Some wrecks don't have a single fish on them."

But with our hopes resting with his extensive underwater knowledge, we set about rigging up gear fit for the task. Editor Mel Russ, myself and England international

shore anglers, Alan Yates and Steve Allmark, were the lads with the task of proving there is still some superb fishing to be had in the North Sea. Our set-ups were quite different, each opting for our favourite rods – Steve with a basic boat rig, Alan an uptider, Mel with his trusty 301b class Shakespeare and myself with a purpose-built Daiwa pirker.

We test the waters...
The throb of the engines finally fell silent as Dave called from the wheelhouse: "Right, we're just uptide of the wreck now."

▲ *A start to some serious fishing, in perfect weather.*

▼ *Yes, there really are cod in the North Sea!*

Dave had skilfully manoeuvred the boat into position to obtain the best possible drift and we were ready, with reels knocked out of gear and thumbs on spools, waiting for action.

As two of the lads had opted for the feathers and pirk approach and Mel had gone for a jelly worm, I thought I'd try for a tiny black Red Gill to ring the changes. This is an important aspect to remember when 'team' fishing. There's no point being a loner when you're on a boat trip because that can only lead to problems and ultimately will reduce the overall catch. If you all try something different, you can evaluate the results as the fish boxes fill up, or remain empty, as the case may be!

A special day

Anyway, it was clear from the first drop that the day was going to be something special. Before I could even feel the lead 'clank' on the metal of the wreck, my rod, a Shimano BeastMaster filled with 35lb superbraid mainline, arched over as a fish hit the lure.

For anyone who has not used braid as a mainline, and I was one of them before

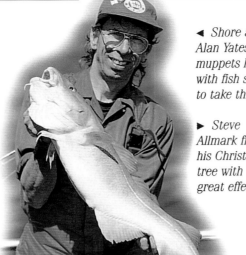

◀ *Shore angler Alan Yates used muppets loaded with fish strip to take this fish.*

▶ *Steve Allmark fished his Christmas tree with great effect!*

this trip, please give it a go. It opens all kinds of doors you never knew existed when playing fish. You feel every lunge, you can work the artificial that much better, you need less lead to hold it against the tide, and most importantly, it's great fun.

After several lunges beneath the boat and a few last gasp darts, my prize languished in the surface layers of the

water, ready to be hauled aboard. Not a cod, but a pollack approaching double-figures. A worthwhile start to a superb day. But things didn't always go to plan. During the morning I managed quite a few fish on the Red Gill and braid approach but during the afternoon I didn't have it all my own way. Mel, standing just feet from me, was bagging up, as was Steve and Alan. Had my Red Gill suddenly developed a bad case of body odour?

I wasn't sure, but the three anglers using pirks, feathers and muppets were making me look a bit of a prat. At one point Steve was catching so well, he had a near double-figure cod on every feather, Alan was pirking like a pro and Mel was giving the cod a real battering by working a string of large white cod feathers above a pound sinker.

The tables had turned. It was as if the fish had decided 'enough was enough' on my rod and it was time to give the other

▼ *The good ship* Que Sera Sera, *ready for the off. Inset at right shows spacious cabin.*

FACT FILE

If you fancy booking a trip out of Ramsgate aboard Dave Barrett's boat, *Que Sera Sera*, give him a call on tel: 01843 580292 or on the boat: 0860 224945. Boat places are £30 per person per day, and the boat will take up to 12 anglers.

▲ *John McKenzie with a couple of prime wreck cod.*

▲ *The Sea Angler team with proof there are cod in the North Sea!*

three guys a go. I kept quiet and just concentrated as fish, after fish, after fish came over the gunnels to my left. Needless to say, the lads were having the time of their lives, very much like me a few hours earlier. Then it struck me what the guys were doing different and must have been the reason for such steady sport. Every time they finished a drift, they hauled in the muppets and pirk, adding a small sliver of fresh mackerel flesh to each of the hooks. This added attraction was the only difference in set-ups and was surely the reason such catch differences were being achieved.

I learnt a lesson the hard way. Watch the more successful anglers on the boat, the baits they use and even the way they work the lure.

Fishing like this is all about interpretation and adapting it to suit you and your kit. If you do it right, and the skipper has done his job, it's just a case of getting on with the fishing.

Simplistic maybe, but why make angling more difficult than it really is? Remember you're trying to catch a cod which has probably never seen a hook, and certainly hasn't got a university degree in avoiding a hook. Looking back, we didn't clean out the wrecks of cod, but how many fish do you really want to catch?

By mid-afternoon four fish boxes were full and it was time to say enough is enough. Conservation is the name of the game, and there's no point catching more than you can carry and leaving half behind. We had more than 300lb of cod between us, and believe me, we struggled to take even half back home!

The trip underlined the fact that anglers must watch, listen, learn and then adapt to every fishing technique until the jackpot is hit. One-method anglers usually end the day with a long face unless they try different tactics.

This was no lucky lottery win, we held the trump cards and just played a winning hand at the right time. Our prize... a codding jackpot!

HOT WRECKING TIPS

◆ When using a Red Gill make sure you don't strike if you feel a fish grab the artificial. The trick is to keep reeling so the fish will then attack and get hooked. Strike, and you could rip the hook straight from its mouth.

◆ If you opt to use braid as a mainline, it's best to use a monofilament leader on the end. This absorbs some of the shock of the fish grabbing the artificial. Make sure you use enough to go up and down the rod, leaving about five turns on the spool.

◆ Pirking requires the angler to work the artificials to get the fish interested. In these situations, a stiffer rod gives you more control and more pulling power.

◆ Most pirks come with a treble hook attached. The skipper, Dave Barrett, recommends that you cut off at least one of the hooks to reduce the chance of snagging the wreck, especially if netting is hanging from it.

◆ Dave has found a lot of the fish have been caught by holding the pirk just off the wreck and letting the tide work it. This is a case of something different sometimes outscoring the normal method.

◆ Don't retrieve your pirk or Red Gill to the surface on every drop. Time is of the essence when drift fishing, so retrieve so far, then drop back to the wreck.

◆ Count the number of reel handle turns you make before you hit fish. This can act as a measure for future drops and save you valuable time.

◆ When dropping down the artificial, don't slow it down. You could find, like us, that mackerel can become a pain in the butt!

Have fork, will travel

On these pages we explain how to collect various baits for free. You can learn about various types of sea bed uncovered by the tide and what to find when you get out there with a fork

WHERE TO LOOK

The best places to dig are usually those that are most sheltered from prevailing winds and sea. Estuaries are full of bait, while bays behind a headland, harbour, creek or even a rocky coast offer places that marine life can get a foothold. It's a fact that even the most barren-looking sand is often full of life.

You can discover the most productive digging spots by touring the coast with your binoculars during a spring low tide. Look for groups digging, because most coasts have an army of professional diggers, along with enthusiastic anglers happy to dig their own bait. The other way is to practice trial and error on venues. This is probably the best way to find those secret spots to get white ragworm. Popular spots have to provide enough bait for the professionals to make a living and they tend to ignore the less productive places. Finding your own spot can keep you supplied with bait for relatively little effort.

THE TIDES

The most important aspect of bait digging is an understanding of the tide so that you get to your mark at low tide.

First step is to get your hands on a tide table for your local region. Some tides go out further than others and it's the spring low tides which are best for bait digging. Study your tide table and you will see the height of the tide alongside the low and high tide times.

Make sure you buy a tide table which shows these details. The National Federation of Sea Anglers diary has all the tide times and heights, plus the constants for ports around the British Isles. So no matter where you live in the UK, you will be able to easily work out the low and high tide times by adding or subtracting the constant that's relevant to your region.

The type of fork that you use is very important, so don't just pick out any old bit of kit that happens to be lurking in the garden shed. What you really need to do is to go out and buy a strong, flat-tined potato fork, by far the best all-round tool for baiting.

Flat-tined forks are best for digging in wet sand and thin-tined ones for digging in stony ground because they penetrate easier, but all-round, the flat-tined type wins hands-down.

Price is a consideration too: a quality make costing slightly more will last for years. So steer clear of cheap tools and beware of curved tines, which can give you backache after a short while. Moulded plastic handles are light and comfortable, but wooden ones can be replaced easily.

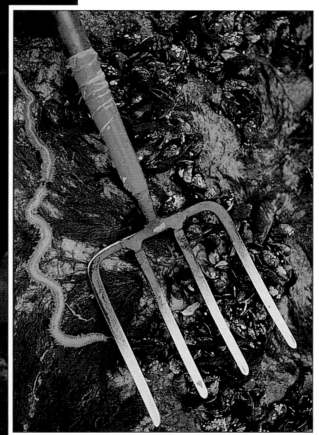

▲ *Flat-tined forks are best for digging in wet sand.*
◄ *Mud, shingle and shale is more likely to be populated by ragworm.*

More bait digging next page ▶

Extremely low spring tides can produce worm, sandeel and shellfish.

GENERAL FORK DIGGING TIPS

◆ Digging worm with a fork doesn't require much technique in most regions. It's a matter of digging as if in the garden.

◆ Sharpening the tines of your digging fork can make digging easier, because a sharp fork will penetrate the sand or mud with less effort. A good professional digger's trick grind down the back of the tines, tapering them to a good point.

◆ Digging tidily in rows with one foot in the row eases back problems and allows you to dig deeper. Keep the water out of your dig with a wall of sand to form a moat for the water to drain off.

◆ It's important to keep your worm cool as you dig. A smaller bucket inside a big one filled with water keeps bait cool because any breeze cools the water. On a hot day you can add a freezer pack to help things along.

◆ Don't mix different worm or damaged ones as most are not compatible. Put a couple of different size ice-cream tubs inside your bucket for the different worm.

◆ Watch for blisters on your hands caused by rough edges on the fork shaft. Wrap a length of PVC tape around the shaft or file any rough edges off before you dig.

◆ Prevailing winds affect the location of worm. Look up the sheltered edges of reefs, groynes and piers, because these are often where worm are gathered by tide and rough seas. Other diggers are less likely to investigate the sand close to obstacles or the high tide line – many simply rush as far out as they can get.

◆ TOP TIP ◆
Remember that when you find the digging difficult, with worm hard to come by, it's likely that there will also be less around in the tackle shops. Dig in advance of your fishing or order back-up bait from a dealer.

CHALK AND SAND

Such terrain produces blow lugworm on the sandbars between the chalk ridges, along with white ragworm in the sand and rockworm in the chalk itself.

The lowest tides often have banks of tube worm. Digging can reveal a number of different marine worm as well as razorfish.

Look close to the high tide line for groups of lugworm washed in by heavy seas. These may be easier to dig because the sand is shallow over chalk rock. Gullies and ledges between the chalk can be full of marine life.

Lugworm from clean sand are often shallower, as well as being thinner-skinned than those from mud – they also require a little more care in hot weather. make sure you purge the sand from the worm by storing them in water and make sure you keep them cool.

◆ TOP TIP ◆
You can break up chalk rock with a fork to reveal rockworm and clam, but watch your eyes for flying splinters of chalk.

FLAT SANDY STORM BEACHES

◆ Flat, featureless storm beaches, where seas pound the inter-tidal region, are the common beaches along east and Atlantic coasts.

◆ Sometimes it is not possible to dig bait from these shorelines, but there are occasions when bait can be collected from the high tide line after a storm.

◆ On a few storm beaches low spring tides show worm, sandeel and shellfish, with big black lugworm the most often found species at the extremities of the beach.

◆ Black lugworm live deep, and are less likely to be dislodged than the common blow lug. They can be dug with fork, spade or pumped, needing more technique than garden-style lugworm digging.

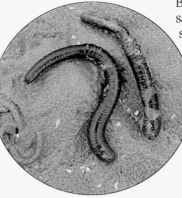

▲ *Sand casts show the location of worms.*

◆ Storm beaches are best in summer, when long, calm spells allow worm numbers to build up.

◆ Flat sands often produce shellfish, sandeel and white ragworm, though stocks do go up and down with storms and weather. Best digging time is when sand is dry, so don't dig too soon: leave until the tide is out and sand drained. Tell-tale casts and marks on the dry surface show the location of a multitude of creatures.

◆ TOP TIP ◆

Try digging close to the base of the shingle for white ragworm, washed there in storms. They often find a safe haven among a hard sea bed mixture of shingle and sand. Patches of tube worm at the extreme low water mark are often home to white ragworm.

MUSSEL BEDS

These areas are often ignored by less experienced worm diggers, although they can contain a treasure-trove of white ragworm, long stringy thin ragworm, and the biggest king ragworm.

Digging in terrain like this can be tedious because the ground is often tough and stony. The best way forward is to run your fork into the mud and stones at a shallow angle and take off the sand and mud close to the surface.

The large king ragworm may be deeper in the hard grey mud, so be ready to grab one smartly if you see it on the retreat down its burrow.

Wading to a mussel island during the spring low tides can result in a bumper dig. Follow the contours of buried rocks when digging around mussel beds, because some diggers give up when they hit stone.

◆ TOP TIP (below) ◆

Draining a pool can be worth the effort. Pile mud and shingle into the water and then stand on the island you have created and dig to expel the water

ESTUARY, SAND AND MUD

It's common to find abundant bait supplies in sheltered estuaries and creeks, but ironically, fewer fish. Collecting bait from such regions is relatively easy with a fork the most appropriate tool.

Sand, mud, shingle or shale mixtures usually offer a plentiful supply of lugworm. Mud, shingle and shale is more likely to be populated by ragworm, both the smallest wriggly harbour ragworm and the largest king ragworm.

The kings are identifiable by a hole, and treading on the mud often produces a spurt of water out of their burrow. Harbour ragworm show thousands of tiny blow holes. King ragworm tend to be deeper as they get bigger. In some regions they can be dug three a fork-full, in others you need to be a miner to dig the biggest worm.

Lots of river estuaries and rivers have harbour ragworm close to the bank, among reeds and grass well inland. In some, you can dig muddies virtually at high water, during the short neap tides.

Digging harbour ragworm can be

messy and dangerous, so test mud banks before you venture on to them. Beware when crossing estuary streams to banks, so that you are not cut off by the tide. Don't venture out into a large estuary in fog unless you are sure of your route; even then you should always carry a compass.

◆ TOP TIP ◆

Keep the hole you dig clear of sand and mud because this allows you to get deeper without placing any strain on the fork handle. Little and often digs are more effective than large forkfuls.

Shell seekers

Little technique is required to collect shellfish, just add stamina and a knowledge of where and when to look. Here we examine ways to collect those used for bait

HUNTING FOR RAZOR FISH

There are two ways to collect razorfish, either by digging or picking them up from the high or low tide marks after a storm. Fairly sheltered sandy beaches are the best places to look, and tube worm or yellowtail lugworm are a clue to the presence of razorfish. They are found mainly at the extreme low tide mark with the lowest spring tides the best time to target them with a fork.

A degree of stealth is required because at the drop of a foot on the sand, the bigger razorfish retreat rapidly down their burrow. Forking them out requires digging two deep spits, although if you are quick enough you will expose the shell on the first dig.

Look for shells sticking out of the sand, or small keyhole shapes in the sand. Look also for the marks made by splashes of water on the sand, produced as razorfish move up and down their burrows.

If you expose a razorfish, grab it, but don't pull too hard otherwise its fleshy foot will grip the sand and be broken off. Keep up a steady, gentle pressure and the shellfish will release its grip on the burrow.

It is possible to raise a razorfish by squirting very salty water down its burrow. A washing-up liquid bottle filled with concentrated saltwater does the trick. The smaller razorfish washed in by the waves rarely have a deep burrow. It's the largest razors that have been established for some time that are most difficult to dig.

Razor burrows often go off at an angle. Don't be too keen to dig deep too quickly because you risk losing the hole. Lots of little digs exposes a razor's shell.

◄ Top: Look for the shell sticking out of the sand.

Middle: Don't pull too hard, otherwise the fleshy foot will be broken off.

Bottom: Keep up a steady, gentle pressure and the shellfish will release its grip on the burrow.

BUTTERFISH

This shellfish has several names, including trough shell and Venus shell and is another common bivalve mollusc, all of which have two halves to their shell.

Many types, in various sizes, are commonly found washed up after a gale. The butterfish lives close to the surface of the sand, so is not difficult to dig. If you visit the low water mark after the sand has dried out, butterfish are often showing on the surface.

Investigate any lump or bump on the surface of the sand and it probabaly turn out to be a butterfish. Lots of tiny shellfish that live in shell grit and sand are food to the flatfish and even the smallest shells can be collected for bait.

COCKLES

Cockles live close to the surface of the sand and can be collected with a fork or a rake. The common cockle is not a very effective bait though, and most anglers tend to ignore it. It's the larger queen cockle which is more highly prized. This has a large, orange, tongue-shaped body. In fact, the meat of such a shellfish is the muscle that closes the shell.

Again, these often gather at the high or low tide mark after having been ripped out of the sandbars by a storm. They tend to live below the low tide mark and those found at low tide are usually the remnants or survivors of a storm which has moved them closer to the shoreline.

◄ *Collect razorfish by either digging them or picking them up from the high or low tide mark.*

More shellfish next page ▶

CLAMS

There are several varieties of clam in different regions around the coast – some big and some small. The two most common and largest are the caper clam and the common clam.

Both are used as bait although, as with most other shellfish, they are more effective when naturally available to the fish after a storm.

You will occasionally come across a large clam while digging for lugworm and ragworm in muddy estuaries, although in some regions they are more plentiful and can be deliberately targeted.

▲ *Piddock clam live in clay and chalk rock.*

▼ *Piddock contain a lot of water and shrink rapidly.*

PIDDOCK CLAM

Piddock clam live in clay and chalk rock and can be dug by breaking off the edges of the clay or chalk. Populations are found where chalk downland and cliffs meet the sea. Petrified forest is also home to piddock clam.

The bigger piddocks burrow deeper and are more difficult to reach if you have to dig directly down to them. Clam shrink rapidly because they contain a lot of water and the smallest are not really worth digging, although they may look large at first sight.

A great bait when frozen, they are also said to be most effective when rotten but the stench is truly unbelievable. Watch your eyes when digging in hard clay or chalk because spurts of water and mud are a problem.

▶ *Bigger piddock clam burrow deeper and are more difficult to reach.*

OTHER SHELLFISH

There are many shellfish varieties off the coast of the British Isles. Here are some more to add to your hunting menu.

MUSSEL

Mussel can be collected from groyne posts and rocks and are occasionally washed up along the shoreline after a storm.

They are an effective bait over mixed ground and rock, and make a very good standby for peeler crab. If you can't find them on the beach, they are also available from the fishmonger – and large, cultivated mussel varieties appear to be just as effective as wild ones.

SLIPPER LIMPET

This shellfish is not native to Britain, but has populated many southern shorelines after having been brought here by the shipping industry.

Groups or strings of slippers stick to stones and can be picked up along the shoreline. They are most effective as bait following a storm when their shells are smashed up by heavy seas.

SCALLOPS

Several varieties of this shellfish can occasionally be found washed up on the low tide mark and all can be used as bait. Scallops are also available from the fishmonger, although they are not widely used as bait, due to their cost.

SHELLFISH DIGGING TIPS

◆ A flat tined fork is ideal for turning over sand and mud to reach shellfish. Keep the hole clear of sand and deliberately follow the burrow. If you appear to miss the shell, fork back over it.

◆ Look closely at the surface of dry sand – the presence of many shellfish is revealed by the tiniest indentations and marks. After you have looked over a stretch of sand it's worth going back for a look later, when the tide is a low ebb, as shellfish are continually coming to the surface.

◆ Keep a close watch on the surface of the mud for those tell-tale spurts of water which are a sure-fire clue that will reveal the location of clam, as well as razorfish.

◆ Digging for razorfish and butterfish is far more effective at dead low water, when the sand begins to dry out – it's at this time when shellfish come to the surface. You can even pick razorfish up with your fingers at night, when they come right out of the sand.

◆ There are several species of razorfish, but you can ignore the big black and bright yellow ones as bait.

◆ After a storm, look at the base or gully close to the downtide side of a groyne, because it's here that dislodged shellfish will end up. A shrimp net pushed through a gully is the way to collect them. The uptide length of long groynes is also the place to find razorfish sticking out of the sand after rough seas.

◆ Look in high tide pools and sandbars on sandy shores with a sand or rock base against promenade or beach for shellfish deposited by rough seas after spring tides.

◆ On a shoreline that is new to you, look for groups of gulls and other seabirds wading or flying close to the tide line, because they provide a clue to the whereabouts of shells washed inshore.

▼ *Slipper limpet stick to stones and can be picked up along the shoreline.*

Great white hope

White ragworm are the top bait when the going gets tough,
so find out how to secure your own supply

White ragworm are principally a match fishing bait. They are favoured by competition anglers when fishing for codling, dogfish, pouting or general scratching for tiddlers when fish are scarce or hard to catch. Whites have a special attraction to small fish and are deadly in poor fishing conditions. There are two basic kinds of white ragworm, the large pearl-coloured snakes and the small wriggly cat whites or sand whites. Both are deadly in their own right, but it is small white ragworm which are most often called upon when fishing is slow. Larger snake whites are more versatile for bigger species.

▶ *White ragworm clean themselves by expelling any sand, so wash them out in fresh sea water several times before you return home.*

WHERE AND WHEN

The two types are found in different places. Large snakes are most often located in mixed shingle, mud and sand and are usually found around mussel beds or tube worm.

Smaller white ragworm are found in almost any kind of clean sand, often among lugworm. This variety can grow fairly large, even rivalling snake white ragworm, but digging has decimated the larger sand whites in most regions.

White ragworm populations fluctuate and they will move if water temperatures alter rapidly or for other reasons. Even over-digging causes them to migrate away from the shore. The advantage is that populations can also suddenly appear or increase over the course of a couple of tides. It is the spring low tide that offers the best chance of getting to the largest populations of white ragworm from most venues. Regular digging at the low tide mark makes it essential to select the lowest of low spring tides.

▲ *Spring low tides offer the best chance of getting to the largest populations of white ragworm from most venues.*

METHODS

Whites need to be dug with a fork. You risk chopping them up if you try using a spade. Wide-tined potato forks are best for sand and thin square tines best for rough or rocky ground.

Make sure that the fork handle is smooth and free from rough metal edges which can cause blisters. Rub these down with a file and cover with tape.

There are no secret methods for digging white ragworm and the basic technique is to dig garden fashion in rows.

The more ground you turn over the greater number of worm you are likely to uncover. However, there are a number of things to look for to improve the results of your efforts. Firstly, concentrations of tube worm usually have more white ragworm in them. The reason for this is that whites are cannibalistic and, apart from eating their own, eat other marine worm as well. Drop a king ragworm in a bucket of whites and watch the panic. Whites tend to be dug in clusters, which also relates to patches of the correct sand, moisture or areas that

have not been dug before. So it is important to move around when digging until you start uncovering worm. Sand worm tend to rise to the surface when digging because the water drains and sometimes they show themselves. In soggy sand in some regions they go deeper and it pays to keep moving to an undisturbed spot after a few rows.

Rocks and stony ground, which are difficult to dig over, have a larger head of whites per square yard. This is simply because some diggers tend to concentrate on the softer, easier ground. Similarly some diggers are expert in draining rock pools where worm have been safe from the fork for some time and have grown large.

Look closely at the ground for signs of previous digging before you dig; soft or

◆ Watch out for fresh water in pools when filling your bucket. It drains into pools after a shower and in some regions comes down the estuary at low tide.

◆ It is best to segregate large and small white ragworm – the larger snake whites will eat the tiddlers. You can feed large whites on small worm, if keeping them for a long time. Ragworm can also be fed on small amounts of crushed trout pellets.

◆ You can dig at night with the aid of a headlamp. Go for a six-volt light with a wide beam. There are obvious dangers of digging at night, so be absolutely sure of your route back to shore and the state and time of tide.

◆ Don't discard cut worm and tails because these can be kept alive in water inside the fridge for several days.

◆ White ragworm can sometimes be found in very shallow sand on a clay base where it's difficult to dig down. Angle your fork, then spoon sand off to get at the worm.

◆ Top spots to dig whites, apart from where there are tube worm, are against groynes and walls where they may congregate after rough weather. Sometimes the joint between the shingle and sand can also be a place to find concentrations; in fact, worm can even be found in the coarse shingle high up the beach.

◆ Find those secret white rag beds by touring the coast during the lowest spring tides. Concentrations of cars on a beach road or diggers out on the sand give the game away.

◆ You may have to work very hard for just a few worm in regions where there is heavy pressure. In places like this, lots of bait diggers automatically go out as far as they can, so don't neglect areas close to the shore. Even so, it can be worth driving further afield.

▲ *Large snake whites are usually found around mussel beds or tube worms.*

soggy ground will be revealed by a prod with the fork. Place the worm in a bucket of clean sea water as you dig. Don't mix dead or damaged worm with whole live ones and don't place different species of worm in the same bucket.

If you are digging lugworm and picking up the odd white ragworm, tack on a small bucket to the side of your main bucket. This ensures that your small quantity of white ragworm will remain in good condition.

You will find that the worm clean themselves out by expelling any sand. So after digging, wash them out in fresh sea water several times before you return back home. For storage you can use two buckets (one inside the other) and you can also take home some fresh, clean seawater for storing your worm in the fridge.

Common lugworm

Worried about your bait presentation? Follow our handy advice and no self-respecting fish will refuse your bait

Common lugworm, sometimes called blow or soft lugworm, are widely available and are the regular choice of bait for most sea anglers. Getting the best from them means several points about digging or buying your supply are worth considering.

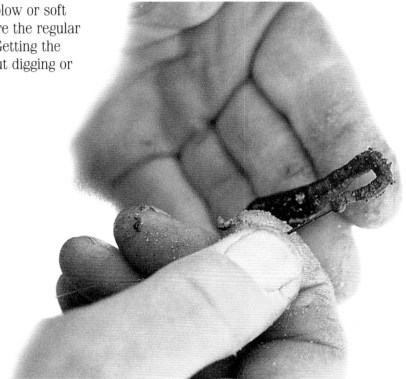

1

SIZE

Lots of sea anglers are obsessed with the need to use only big lugworm. This stems mostly from their instinct for obtaining value for money. However, more important is grading the size of the worm to the type of fishing and fish sought.

Big worm are ideal when boat fishing for cod, but for shore fishing, for say codling and flatfish, then small ones are far more effective.

Think about their size in relation to the fish you seek before buying. Consider that several small worm have a longer lasting scent trail than a single large worm. Large ones may be more economical, but tend to lose their scent faster.

QUALITY

Quality is really important, because lugworm can produce a wide range of results relating to their age and the type of sea bed they come from.

Older worm seem to be more effective on most occasions, while those from different types of sand and mud definitely bring rather varied results.

Try carrying out some trial and error experiments with specimens you have caught in your region – you might find these throw up a few surprises!

TOP TIPS

◆ Don't pre-bait lugworm too early before casting a spare baited rig. If you do, the scent and blood will drain from them.

◆ Lugworm shrink after going on the hook, so allow for this when deciding bait size.

◆ If using bait clips, you will need a bait stop which must be pulled down the hook snood to secure the threaded worm.

◆ When you are baiting with large numbers of small lugworm, use a second hook sliding on the snood above the normal hook. This is called a Pennell rig and it helps secure the bait up the snood. It also ensures that, whichever end the fish takes, it will be able to find a hook.

◆ Renew lugworm baits after every cast; they soon wash out and lose vital blood and scent.

◆ Most of the more common fish species respond to lugworm with a tipping bait. You can add a small piece of squid, fish or ragworm to achieve better results on those occasions when the action seems to be rather slow.

◆ Small lugworm can be fished in bunches for species such as flounder. You can also bait them so that the tails can move in an enticing way.

STEP-BY-STEP

1 First step when baiting lugworm is to remove the sandy tail. You can then thread its head or tail first on to the point of the hook.

2 If you puncture the worm when doing this, don't worry because this allows blood and scent to escape. Varying the number of puncture holes in the worm alters the bait's scent trail.

3 Opinions differ on whether it is best to thread them head or tail first, although the majority of sea anglers reckon that threading the worm tail first, so that the hook point is the bloodiest end, is more likely to result in a hooked fish.

4 It is easier to thread a worm on a long-shanked hook. Grip the worm by the end and push it on to the hook point, threading slowly. Make sure the hook goes through the centre of the worm.

5 Loops hanging from the hook allow a worm to sag and give the fish something to grab and pull the worm off.

6 Aim to thread the worm completely on to the hook and snood.

7 If you find this difficult then a baiting needle is the answer.

8 Thread the worm on to this, then insert the hook point in the end of the baiting needle and push the worm down the needle and around the hook bend.

9 Here the lugworm is threaded and ready to go!

King ragworm

More tips on bait presentation, this time featuring a brightly-coloured and richly-scented member of the worm family

King ragworm are the largest of the ragworm family and available either freshly dug or farmed. Baiting them on the hook depends on their size, with varying ones available.

SIZE

Buying by weight is considered more economical than number, but always ask for the size of worm you require to suit the fish you seek. Dealers will not necessarily supply one size with most offering a mixture.

You want several small wriggling ragworm for flounder and plaice, while a large juicy king is needed for bass, and a section of a large one for pouting and dogfish.

QUALITY

You need good quality bait, so watch for tanked worms which may be anaemic-looking and washed free of most of their scent or flavour. Some dealers store their worm in water inside a fridge and this washes out the digested mud. This can make them less attractive to the fish, as well as slippery to hold when baiting.

Fresh worm are usually bright red and oozing juices. You can toughen up and enhance the colour of tanked ragworm overnight by wrapping them in newspaper.

▶ *Tip off ragworm with other baits, and other ragworm species, including whites.*

TOP TIPS

◆ For most worm baits, Aberdeen hooks are best. They are easier to hold while threading the worm on to the hook. Size 2s are ideal for small ragworm aimed at flounder and 2/0 upwards for bass and larger species. Ragworm have sharp pincers so make sure you thread and grip them tightly.

◆ Although ragworm are often large and tough, they shrink rapidly in water on the hook. The golden rule to follow with this bait is never to bait with just one small worm. Remember to use bigger ones or bait them in bunches.

◆ You can buy farmed ragworm from your tackle dealer, or direct from: Seabait Ltd, Woodhorn Village, Ashington, Northumberland NE63 9NW, tel/fax: (01670) 814102. The big advantage of these is that you can buy the size you want and they keep alive for at least a week.

◆ Dunking a worm's tail in water stops it breaking off during casting. You should renew ragworm baits every cast.

◆ You can tip off ragworm with other baits, just like lugworm. Ragworm lends itself to a section of sandeel, peeler crab and mackerel, as well as the other species of ragworm including whites.

◆ Definitely one of the best ways to deter those pesky bait-robbing shore crab is the head section of a large king ragworm. All you need to do is simply hook the head on the hook bend. Hooks with bait barbs are ideal.

◆ The number of times you penetrate the worm's skin with the hook point alters the flow of scent. One angler we know who does well with this bait cuts the worm into short lengths and then threads them on the hook crossways to increase the flow of scent and juices.

◆ Drop a wet slippery ragworm in the sand to give you added grip when baiting.

HOOKING A RAGWORM STEP-BY-STEP

S elect the bait you require on the hook. Two or three small worm are usually better than a single large one, because this combination offers more movement and a longer lasting scent trail.

Grip the worm near the head. When it opens its mouth to reveal the pincers, pass the hook point into its mouth and then through its body. You can bring the point out an inch or so from the tail to allow the tail to wriggle. Repeat this with all the selected bait. You can thread one or more of them partially, so that a wriggling tail hangs below the bait as an extra attractor, for large flounder or plaice baits.

Multi-ragworm baits are intended to have several tails hanging as attractors. Use a baiting needle if you have trouble holding and threading ragworm on the hook. There are several sizes of needle, with a finer, bendy version more efficient for threading through smaller ragworm.

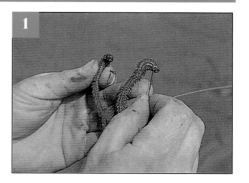

▲ **1-3** Pass the hook point into the mouth and then through the worm's body. Bring the point out an inch or so from the tail to allow the tail to wriggle attractively. Repeat this with one or more worm.

▲ *Fresh worm are usually bright red and oozing juices. These are good specimens.*

BEWARE

◆ Mind the pincers when using ragworm or removing the washed out bait because they are still active and can give you a nip.

◆ Ragworm juices are very strong and can cause considerable pain if they get into cuts on your hands.

Harbour ragworm

They may be small, but they are an excellent way to achieve good results in match fishing from piers, harbours and estuaries

I f you've ever been confused about bait, then the last thing you need are loads of names for the same thing, however the harbour ragworm falls annoyingly neatly into this category.

You may know ragworm as muddies, maddies, reds or just plain harbours, and there may be other nicknames that would not pass the censor. Angling seems full of these confusions.

Ragworm are used mainly as a match fishing bait for pier, harbour and estuary species.

SIZE

B aiting harbour ragworm can be a fiddly business, because they are small, and many anglers regularly use a baiting needle for this reason. Various sizes of baiting needle are available, but the largest, thickest needles designed for lugworm are far less effective for harbour ragworm.

Being thinner and more active, these worm require a finer, more flexible needle that can be worked completely through their bodies.

HOOKS

T he most popular hooks for baiting harbour ragworm are long-shank Aberdeens, those with a small eye being the most efficient.

Tied with a small half-blood knot in 15lb line, they allow threading of the bait without too much damage, which helps retain them on the hook.

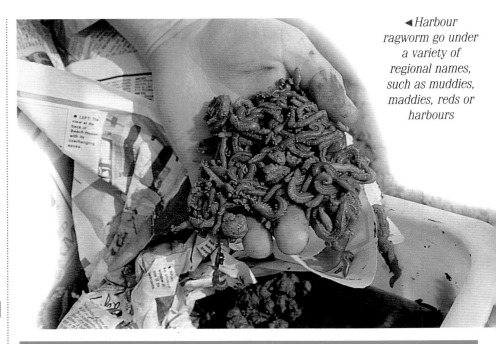

◄ Harbour ragworm go under a variety of regional names, such as muddies, maddies, reds or harbours

TOP TIPS

◆ Maddies are difficult to grip when you are trying to put them on the hook. Drop them in dry sand before threading them on the hook or needle because this provides grip. Storing them in dry sand or vermiculite has the same effect.

◆ Harbour ragworm fish best in large bunches, so take enough when you go fishing. Remember a bunch constitutes wriggly tails, some of which may be lost in the quest to attract fish either by smaller fish biting them off or a few tails flying off when you cast.

◆ One way to overcome tails flying off when you cast is to dunk the finished bait in water. This binds worm tails together.

◆ You don't have to completely renew the bait every cast. They are small enough just to add more. Recharge the hook if it contains only washed out and lifeless remnants.

◆ Fish respond to the wriggling tails, but moving of the hook bait is also a worthwhile tactic.

◆ Single harbour ragworm can work when fished freeline-style for pier, pollack, scad, mackerel and mullet. Adding a few to bread aimed at mullet succeeds in a rough sea.

◆ This bait is extremely robust. Store leftovers in a tray of seawater in a fridge. Then place in newspaper to toughen them up the night before you go fishing.

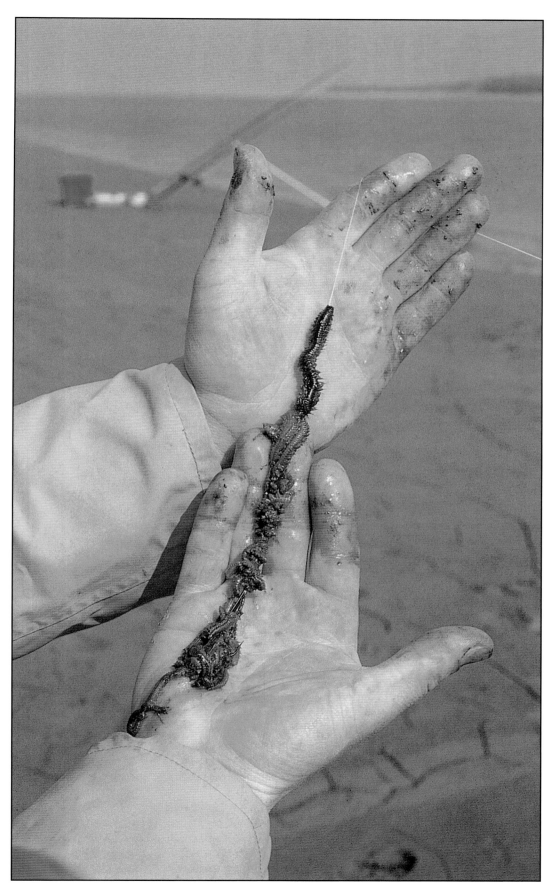

You will need a long-shank hook for baiting without a baiting needle. A size 1, 2 or 4 is the most common choice for flatfish.

Grip the worm by the head and insert the hook point in that end. Thread the first worm on the hook whole, push it around the bend and up over the hook shank, eye and snood. Thread the second, just through the head or half the body, thread the next one whole and repeat the process.

A combination of whole and head-hooked worm produces a large bunched bait that will stay intact. After you have made the bait, pull them gently down towards the hook so the bulk of the bait is on the hook shank and bend.

Ten is the standard hook load for flounder, but you can make up baits with other baits, like lugworm and ragworm, using the harbour ragworm as a cocktail tip. Five maddies on the end of a small king ragworm makes a super flounder bait.

Pre-baited harbour ragworm can quickly die on the hook, so you need careful timing of the preparation of the rig and bait for the next cast.

A baiting needle is absolutely essential for short-shank hooks.

◄ *Ready for action, with a bait presentation that'll have fish leaping out of the water with greed.*

Sandeel

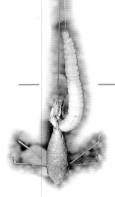

Sandeel has really come into its own as prime bait. This has been fuelled largely by the widespread introduction of top-quality fresh-frozen meat

Baiting with sandeel varies dramatically around the country. Some say you must not burst the belly, others reckon that you shouldn't use bait elastic, or that the eel should be baited tail first, instead of head first. So here we look carefully at the question of just what the best ways are to use the sandeel as bait.

Sandeel can be used fresh or frozen, but it's the latter that has brought them within easy reach of the majority of shore anglers. And it's not only availability that counts, for top quality eel is widely available from the frozen bait lockers.

QUALITY

Quality of sandeel is of vital importance, as it's this factor that makes them easy to put on the hook.

Soft or decaying sandeel really cannot be presented correctly. Sandeel in this state usually end up as an unpleasant and messy mush around the hook, so there is no comparison to be made with top-class fresh frozen eel.

So it's not only essential to start off with the best quality eel, but you need to keep them in that state, too. While they are still frozen, store them in a vacuum flask or cool bag to keep them good and hard, until you are ready to use them.

Even then, your best policy is to remove only a few at a time, just enough sandeels for each cast.

SIZE

The size of the sandeel you use is vitally important, too. Smaller sandeel are best if you plan to go match fishing for dogfish and whiting, while larger specimens are more suitable if you aim to go hunting after bigger fish such as bass, bull huss, ray, tope and pollack.

Remember to match the hook size to the eel you are using and don't use too small a hook, either.

So far as hooks sizes go, a size 1 Aberdeen hook is the minimum you require for a small sandeel – a hook size 1/0 is the one to go for.

For bigger sandeel, an Aberdeen size 2/0 to 6/0 is the perfect solution, with the Kamasan B940 being one of the strongest and sharpest patterns.

TOP TIPS

◆ Sandeel deteriorate in the sun quickly so don't bait up too early and leave baits dangling on a rig in the sun – a tip is to bait up and then return hook baits to your cool bag or box.

◆ Use a baiting needle if you have difficulty threading sandeel around the hook. Also, you can freeze the sandeel down already threaded on a hook and snood. This way you can take your time threading them on the hook carefully.

◆ Most attractive part of the bigger sandeel is the belly, especially if its full of spawn. Pierce or cut the belly section out and mount on the hook. You can also use odd heads and tails to tip off other baits.

◆ If you only have small sandeel, whip several together around the hook to produce a bigger bait.

◆ Pollack are suckers for a spun frozen sandeel and it doesn't matter whether you mount it head or tail first. Thread the hook through the length of the eel and then secure the head or tail with a half hitch in the snood line or a wrap of elastic cotton.

◆ When threading frozen sandeel on head first, push the hook point through the eel's mouth or eye.

◆ Live sandeel do not work so well for the bottom species when shore fishing. They are best used on a float or freeline set up. Simply hook them lightly through the tail so they remain alive and kicking, rather than threading the hook through them.

◆ Frozen sandeel retrieved after a cast may look okay, but they will have lost vital scent and juices, so change them for fresh every cast.

◆ Try adding a sliver of fresh mackerel to a sandeel bait for added scent and colour.

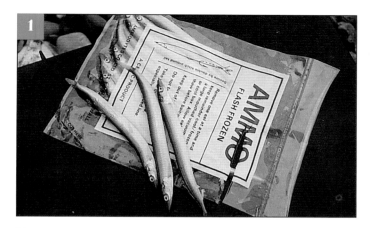

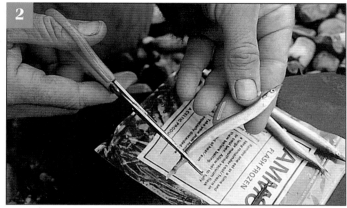

GETTING BAITED

First, remove the sandeel from your flask and warm slightly with your hands. Run the sandeel through your fingers, warming and gradually bending it until it's thawed enough to be threaded around the hook bend. Make sure you don't thaw out the eel too early as it will then be too soft.

You can thread the eel head or tail first. Some anglers cut off the tail, the head, or both.

Carefully thread the hook through the eel without allowing it to cut or pierce the belly or skin. Leave the hook point inside the eel so the tail or head is curved around the hook bend and point.

Once this is done you can add elastic cotton to secure the eel or you can secure it underneath a bait clip. Elastic used to be frowned on, but a few turns around a bait are virtually undetectable.

Variations of the baiting procedure include stabbing the belly of the eel to allow juices to escape more rapidly. Getting the best result is a matter of trying out different approaches.

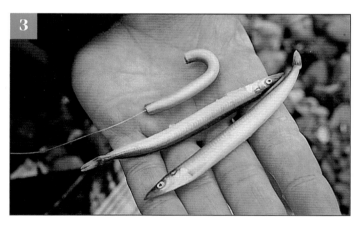

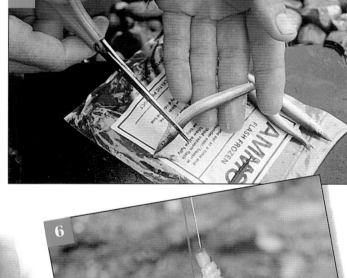

STEP-BY-STEP

1 Frozen sandeel has brought the bait within reach of most shore anglers.

2 Some anglers reckon cutting off the tail works well .

3 Ready to go – this sandeel has had its head and tail removed.

4 The head can be removed like this.

5 Thread the hook through the eel without letting it cut or pierce the belly or skin.

6 Now leave the hook point inside the eel, so that the tail or head is curved around the hook bend and point.

Whole calamari squid

To many people, calamari is something you expect to eat on a vacation in the Mediterranean region. To keen anglers, this squid is one of the best baits available

Squid is just about the most effectively-sized bait for big fish and suits hooks from size 3/0 up to 6/0. It offers the perfect hook and bait combination for species like cod, bass and ray.

Bigger fish can be targeted with larger whole squid or several small ones mounted together.

QUALITY

Although hungry fish crowded around a deepwater wreck may accept smelly squid, lots of shore species definitely prefer the freshest version, so frshness is vital.

Stale squid is betrayed by a pink tinge in the skin and flesh. At worst, the actual flesh is bright pink with a smell that's hard to disregard.

Much of the scent to a squid bait relates to the gut and head section and so fishing them whole and puncturing the gut with the hook releases juices and scents. However, this quickly becomes washed out, despite the bait looking unchanged. It is a good policy to change squid baits fairly regularly if they remain untouched for a half an hour or more.

Once thawed, frozen squid baits lose their freshness rapidly and it is good policy not to return thawed squid to the freezer.

SIZE

The boxed calamari squid, which is imported to the UK, averages eight inches in length, including tentacles. You can purchase boxes with mixed sizes of squid from tackle dealers and supermarkets, but the smallest is rarely less than four inches and the biggest more than nine.

Larger squid are available from fishmongers with the English variety, which is often caught by local trawlers, anything up to 24 inches in length. Cuttlefish are a different variety and available in various sizes. The average is 18in which is too big to use whole except for perhaps very big conger eel.

▶ *Whole squid prepared for shark fishing.*

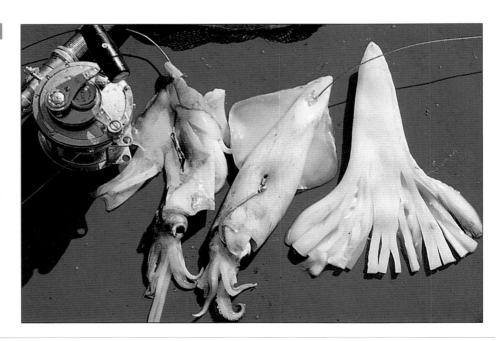

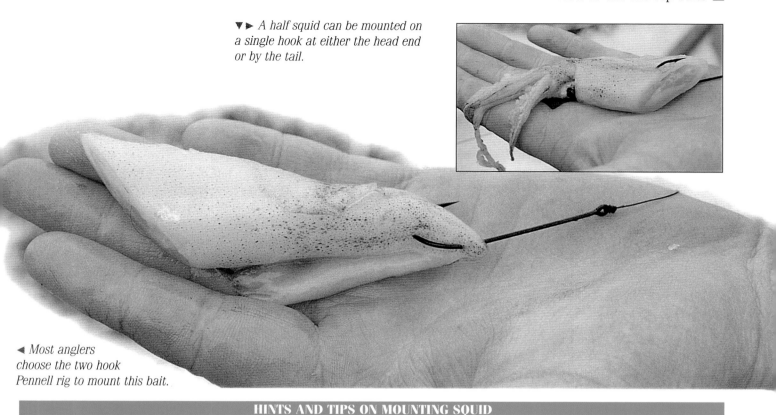

▼▶ A half squid can be mounted on a single hook at either the head end or by the tail.

◄ *Most anglers choose the two hook Pennell rig to mount this bait.*

HINTS AND TIPS ON MOUNTING SQUID

There are a variety of ways to mount squid. Most anglers choose the two hook, Pennell rig to mount this bait.

The Pennell involves one hook on the end of the snood and another hook sliding on the snood by its eye. In some cases a length of plastic tube is added to secure the sliding hook's shank to the snood. The Pennell system is ideal for baiting large baits, such as whole or multiples of calamari squid. This is because the bait can be secured and supported by the main hook at the end of the snood, while the sliding hook helps to support the bait.

Baiting a whole squid on a single hook allows the squid to bunch up around the shank and point of the hook and negate the point's efficiency.

The first step in baiting a squid on a Pennell is to pass the hook completely through the back end of the squid, near the two small fins at the opposite end from the head.

Then wrap the snood line once around the body of the squid and take the hook completely through. Repeat this and then take the hook through the head of the squid, ending with the point protruding between the eyes.

By pulling the snood line tight, you will find that the bait is securely fixed to the hook and snood. You can add a few turns of lightweight elastic cotton if the squid is large or your attempt a bit untidy.

Then take the sliding hook down the snood close to the top of the bait, twist the line around the hook shank a couple of times and then pass it through the bait near the small fins. The sliding hook will then be almost free from the bait, but providing a hook which will catch any big fish taking it.

Two or three squid can be mounted on the rig in a similar way. Make sure they are supported on the hook snood and not allowed to sag or fall around the point. If this has happened when you retrieve the bait, take it off and put on another.

Single hooks can be used if the squid is cut in half or into strips or various portions.

TOP TIPS

◆ Remember that you should not thaw out a whole box of squid and then just leave them laying around in the sun to spoil. It's important to store the squid in a cool bag or box, which will help keep them in top condition, ready for bait preparation.

◆ Removing the skin from the calamari squid reveals attractive white flesh that is a real temptation to hungry fish. An easy way to do this is to grip the two small fins at the top end of the squid's body, and then twist and pull firmly down. You will find that the skin peels off easily, just like that of a banana.

◆ Leave a tag of line off the knot on the bottom hook of the Pennell and this will help secure the bait. You can also use the eye and knot tag positioned in the head of the squid to give added security to this bait.

◆ Don't be tempted to just add another squid to a large squid bait aimed at cod. Make sure that you take the time to remove the old bait and then start again from scratch. If you don't, you risk ending up with a large bait with the hook buried somewhere in the centre.

◆ Save yourself valuable time by baiting up multi-squid baits. Use a spare trace and bait this up between casts.

Fish strip

Did you know that for record-breaking catches, you can't beat a fish bait? If you doubt this, just look at what the British and Irish champions use!

Many anglers ignore fish baits, often preferring the easier-to-hook marine worm. But are they aware that more British and Irish records are held by fish baits than any other type? Perhaps this knowledge will prompt you to give fish a try, especially from a boat, where fresh mackerel is most often available.

The biggest pitfall of using fish baits is to block out the hook by using too much bait, loaded on too small a hook. Blobs of fish will lead to missed bites and frustration, so read on for the very best ways to present this deadly bait.

◄ *Frozen or larger side fillets need to be threaded on the hook and then secured above the eye with bait elastic.*

► *Don't cut too many strips or slivers of bait, especially if you have a limited supply of mackerel.*

SIZE

A strip or fillet of fish on the hook prior to casting can look perfect, but once in the sea it can easily end up like a soggy banana. It will be a mushy mess that will not only be unattractive to the fish but will also impede the hook point's penetration and performance.

To get things perfect for eager bites, the first essential of using fish strip is to match the size of the hook to the size of bait. As a general guide, for normal shore fishing with size 1 or 2 hooks, you need only a thumbnail-size piece of herring or an inch-long sliver of fresh mackerel.

A size 2/0 hook and bigger slice, cutlet or fillet of fish is perfect for boat fishing, but don't be tempted to go too big. The larger fish baits, such as whole side fillets or flappers, are much better suited to a two-hook Pennell rig.

Fish baits are really superb in cocktail form, and a small sliver or strip of one variety added to another bait can serve to increase the likelihood of a bite, For the temptations of a tasty variety can lead greedy fish to a hook very quickly – leading to one of those fishing sessions that anglers all too often only dream about.

QUALITY

The prime essential of using fish baits is that they are fresh. Mackerel and herring need to be fresh and firm. Mackerel left in the sun for a couple of hours deteriorates rapidly, so beware of this and look after your fish.

Frozen fish can be used, but unless it is blast-frozen it is most likely to be softer than fresh. Fresh mackerel oozes blood and the skin will be tough. Herring and sprats are a softer fish bait and again are best used fresh. They may need the assistance of bait elastic though, to hold them in place when thawed out.

◄ *Mackerel fillets ready for use. The head and tail can be used as groundbait.*

▼ *Herring and sprats are a softer fish bait and are best used fresh.*

BAITING UP FISH

There are two ways to bait with fish strip. By far the most effective is to simply pass the hook point through the bait once. This works well with fresh mackerel, because the skin is tough and holds the bait in position, even when power casting.

For herring, sprat or softer fish baits like frozen mackerel, you have to pass the hook point in and out of the bait several times.

Secure the bait with several warps of elastic bait cotton around the snood line above the hook eye. Hooks with shank barbs are preferred by some anglers to help hold such baits in position.

Larger side fillets need to be threaded on the hook, then secured above the eye.

Don't pass the hook completely through the length of the bait or it will slip down the snood. Just pass the length of the hook through that much of the bait and then secure it with cotton.

▲ *Add a small sliver or strip of fish to another bait to form a cocktail.*

TOP TIPS

◆ Although you will need a sharp knife to fillet fish baits, like mackerel and herring, a pair of scissors is a more efficient method for cutting up bait-size strips and slivers. You can also trim fish baits with the scissors after they have been hooked.

◆ A popular way of toughening up mackerel and herring strip or use when distance casting is to salt it down the night prior to fishing. This removes the moisture and dries the bait out making it extremely tough. It starts to soften up on hitting the sea bed.

◆ The thickness of a fish fillet affects the size of the sliver or strip. If you are stuck with large fresh mackerel, slice some of the meat off the fillet, particularly from the belly to make the fish strip more manageable.

◆ You can also taper the fish strip so that the blunt end is placed on the hook tailing off to a point. This works well for fishing for garfish, scad and mackerel because the sliver then resembles a small fish or sandeel.

◆ If you forget a cutting board to cut your bait, don't ruin your knife by cutting on concrete or stone. Try turning your bucket upside down and use the bottom Be warned though, some people think it is unlucky!

◆ Don't cut too many strips or slivers of bait, especially if you have a limited supply of mackerel. Take a fillet off the fish and then store the rest in a cool place or it will deteriorate in the sun or dry out in the wind.

◆ The head and tail of the fish can be cut up and used as groundbait by boat or pier anglers.

Live fish

Many fish can hardly resist a well presented bait that's alive and wriggling. Here are the best ways to get those livebaits on the hook

When you come to think about it, using livebait makes more sense than almost anything else. After all, bass and cod are used to catching their meals alive; it's only scavenger fish varieties which look for dead food naturally. So you can see why livebaiting is an obvious way to go fishing, and success rates tend to be high. It's true, however, that some people think hooking up live creatures as bait is unnecessarily cruel. It's a debate that continues, but the decision is up to you.

◄ *A small baited hook can be attached to the main hook to catch a livebait. A cod is caught on the big hook when it engulfs the livebait.*

▲ *Place the Pennell hooks near the tail or dorsal fins and through the nose, so that they do not impede the bait's movement. You can also leave one hook completely free.*

SIZE

This is the first priority, although so often you have to compromise and use what is available. This can mean using a livebait considered too big.

Livebaits are used for bass and cod. Both readily accept an eight-inch pouting, poor cod or whiting. Bass also take live joey mackerel or sandeel and the use of these baits is limited only to availability of the bait.

Size of the livebait is crucial for winter cod, when shore fishing and casting are involved. Many anglers prefer to fish a double-hook rig, which includes a small baited hook in the attempt to catch a livebait. This is then taken in turn by a cod. This is a method that works, although a major problem is that your unseen livebait can turn out to be too big – a flatfish, 2lb codling, even a dogfish.

It is better to use a small fish, which is cast out. Again, the size is crucial to casting distance.

QUALITY

While a fresh, live fish is the obvious first choice there is a problem. The impact of it landing in the sea after a cast and being dragged to the sea bed by the rig can take its toll.

The first consideration to maintain livebait quality is to fish at short range, so casting is not needed.

For bass, simply lower livebait over the pier wall or drop it behind the breakers after dark. It can be allowed to drift freeline in the tide from the boat.

For cod, get the bait further from the shore. Get it to the sea bed from the boat.

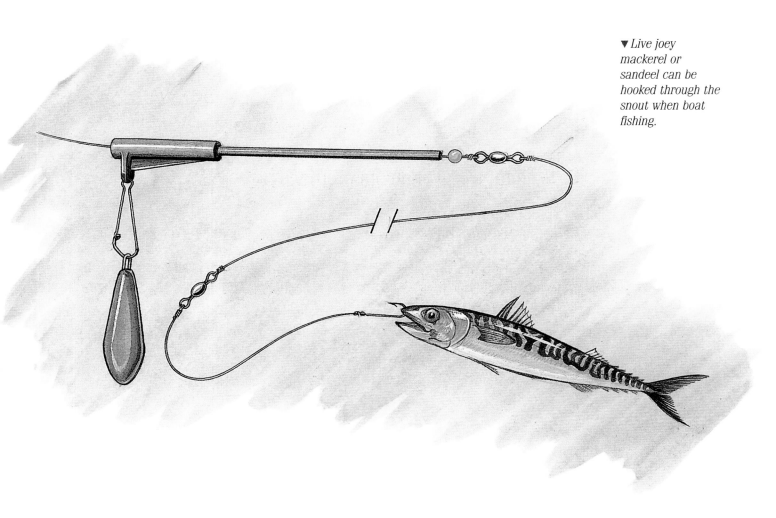

▼ *Live joey mackerel or sandeel can be hooked through the snout when boat fishing.*

BAITING UP LIVE FISH

Although there are a variety of ways of baiting a livebait, lots of anglers prefer a Pennell rig. Place the hooks near the tail or dorsal fins and through the nose, so that they do not impede the bait's movement. You can also leave one hook completely free.

Remember when a fish is hooked tail first it will be drowned on the retrieve, so limit retrieves if you have few baits.

An alternative is to hook the livebait through the wrist of the tail with a single large hook around size 5/0-plus. This avoids the head and vital organs meaning the fish lives longer. Take special care when passing the hook through the tail so that you don't squeeze or damage it. You can also pass the hook through the mouth of a fish.

Live joey mackerel or sandeel can be hooked through the snout.

TOP TIPS

◆ The best conditions for livebaiting from the shore are in the calm, clear water that is available during a spring tide and under a moon.

◆ Keep your livebaits in a bucket with portable pump and air stone. Several tackle firms produce a system specifically for livebaits.

◆ Why not fish with a second rod to catch your live fish?

◆ Fishing a livebait at short range is risky because takes from bass are often sudden and powerful enough to pull the rod into the sea. Set the reel's ratchet or drag, or secure the rod.

◆ Cod tend to carry on feeding as they swallow a small fish. Bites are unpredicatble – they may be either gentle or powerful. Don't strike too quick, but let the cod take the bait.

◆ Watch the rod tip closely. The bait can sometimes signal the imminence of a strike when it panics as a big predator approaches. This panic is what makes the method so deadly efficient, when compared to using a dead fish.

◆ Sometimes a livebait gets jammed in the teeth at the back of a cod's throat without getting a hook-hold. So take it gently and be ready with net because a fish under pressure may eject the bait at the last minute.

◆ Live baiting is considered barbaric by some anglers. Use a deadbait if the idea really bothers you, because it will still catch fish.

Mussels

Mussels are available in a wide variety of sizes and colours. They make an easy-to-obtain bait that is suitable for many different fish species

Mussels are the most convenient of shellfish baits, with both wild and cultivated varieties easily available from fishmongers everywhere. Mussels are also relatively common along the shoreline, although wild ones do tend to be smaller inshore.

Despite the fact that mussels have a regional popularity for cod and coalfish, they can be used to catch lots of different fish species.

▲ *The two places that the shellfish is secured to its shell are cut through with the knife.*

SIZE AND QUALITY

The size of a mussel's shell dictates how much flesh there is inside – the bigger the shell, the more flesh available. The largest mussel varieties are those from Ireland and Scotland, which thrive in the clean rich sea waters.

English wild shoreline mussels are often too small and carry less value as bait; they are also polluted in some regions of the UK.

The cultivated and wild mussel varieties that are sold in fishmongers have invariably been through a filter to purge them of any impurities, though this does not appear to affect their attraction to fish as bait. The largest wild Irish mussels, which are coloured bright orange and yellow, can hardly be compared with some of the more anaemic English shoreline varieties. Colour and scent does vary with the different varieties.

Look for the largest shells you can buy and ensure they are closed tightly, especially if you also wish to eat some.

BAITING UP MUSSELS

The first essential of using mussel on the hook is getting the flesh out of the shell. This requires some dexterity with a blunt-ended dinner knife. Insert the knife in the rear hinge of the shellfish and twist, forcing the two sides apart. Then run the rounded knife blade around the two shells to remove the flesh.

The two places that the shellfish is secured to its shell are cut through with the knife. If you've got the method correct, the flesh will come straight out of the shell in a complete mussel shape, ready to lash on to the hook.

First attempts may break the shape of the flesh, but perfection comes with practise. If you do experience trouble then shell a few mussels before setting out on a fishing session rather than doing this when the fish are biting.

Once you have shelled your mussel you can place a baiting needle through its length and tie it to the needle with wraps of light elastic bait cotton. Then remove the needle and you have a ready available bait. This can then be cut into small pieces for tipping.

You can also lash the mussel directly to the hook again using shearing elastic. Make sure you use plenty of turns to secure the meat firmly, as the flesh is very soft. You can save time by tying the bait onto a number of bait needles or lengths of wire prior to your trip.

◆ The tough foot of the shellfish is small but it will help secure the bait on the hook so pass the hook through it when baiting up.

◆ Mussels can be kept alive very easily in a bucket or plastic box in the fridge. Give them a regular drink of fresh sea water. They thrive in a sack hung over the gunnel rail of the boat.

◆ One of the most effective uses of mussel as bait is in places where peeler crab is a first choice bait. Mussel has a similar scent and scent trail quality as crab and attracts similar responses from the same species.

◆ Frozen mussels are also an effective hook bait and have a much more rapidly dispersing scent trail than fresh. Great as a standby hook bait and also ideal for free offerings.

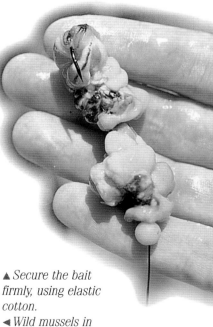

▲ *Secure the bait firmly, using elastic cotton.*
◄ *Wild mussels in their natural habitat.*

White ragworm

These worm are hard to find in some areas,
so anglers tend to be grateful for what
they can get, big or small

▲ *You can use
white ragworm as
an excellent tipping
bait, so they hang
enticingly from the
hook.*

SIZE

Size is rarely an option because white ragworm are
available in only small numbers in many regions of
Britain. Dig your own for a selection of large and small
worms, although in lots of places it is possible to target
large or small worms by digging in specific places.

The large pearly-coloured snake whites are
favoured for codling and dogfish, with an eight-inch
one considered a big one. Pressure of digging does
reduce the average size.

Smaller cat worms (average size four inches) are
more widely available, these being
dug in sand. They
are a
favourite
of the
match
angler for
smaller
species,
such as
pouting,
flounders and
poor cod.

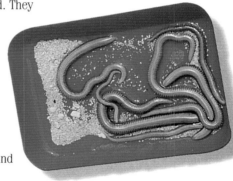

QUALITY

If you buy white ragworm they should be alive in sea
water, not dead wrapped in newspaper. They
deteriorate rapidly when dead and smell rotten. The
only way to keep them alive and in good condition is in
sea water in a fridge.

Their smell is a give away to quality. When they
are sick, they smell like it. Worms tails start to melt
and their tongues pop out when they are in poor
condition. There is nothing you can do to halt their
deterioration. Don't mix whites with other worms
because the juices of lugworms will kill them.

BAITING UP WHITES

You have a choice with white ragworm to
thread them whole on the hook, or do
them like lugworm, in pieces. A favourite
way that experienced anglers bait smaller
worms is in bunches, so that the tails can
be left to wriggle.

Whites do have quite a tendency to
break in half if you try to thread the hook
completely through them. For a wriggly
(and so very attractive) bait, it is better
simply to hook them through the head only.

Remember to remove the tough tongue
of the large snakes first. This makes them
much easier to thread on the hook.

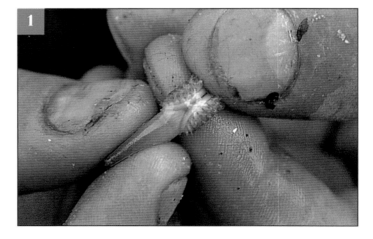

1 First, remove
the worm's tongue
before hooking.
2 This picture
shows the worm
with its tongue
removed.
3 Now thread the
worm up the hook
and snood.

◆ Dunk a bunch of whites in water before you cast. This prevents the tails from breaking off during the cast and ensures a wriggling bait gets to the fish.

◆ Small-eyed hooks enable white ragworm to be threaded up the shank and snood with minimum damage. For small fish, models like Tony's Tackle blues are ideal. The Kamasan B940 is a most suitable pattern for the bigger species.

◆ A plastic bottle is ideal for storing a small supply of white ragworm during a fishing trip. Fill it completely with sea water and screw the cap down tight and the worms will remain safe until they are needed.

◆ If you use a bucket or box they can be split or squashed.

◆ The tail end of a white ragworm is a super tip bait when match fishing. Add it to ragworm, lugworm, peeler or fish. Dabs love just a short section of white ragworm threaded on the end of a lugworm.

◀ *White ragworms on the hook.*

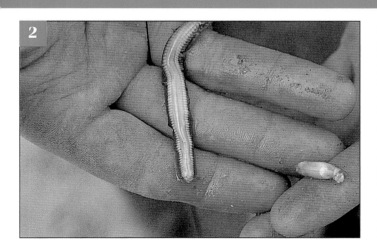

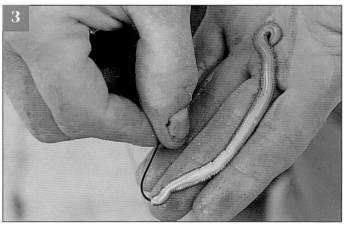

Peeler crab

Crabs make excellent bait, and the average size is a handy two inches or so across the back

◄ *A peeler crab must be just about to shed its shell.*

QUALITY

This is the most important aspect of this bait. They must be just about to shed their shell. At this time they are completely soft internally and their juices are at their most pungent.

Crabs which are ready to use are easy to peel. A good test is that you can actually crush the shell of a claw with your finger and thumb. If a crab is difficult to peel then it is not suitable.

Maintain the quality of your crabs by storing them inside the fridge. This effectively delays the peeling process, which is useful if you don't need to use the peelers for a few days.

Dead crabs are absolutely no use for bait. Peeler deteriorates rapidly once it is dead and appears to lose its appeal to fish. Throw away any dead crabs; saving it for use is a false economy.

SIZE

A common shore crab has to shed its shell to grow, which means most peeler crabs fall into a particular size band. Crabs of around two inches across the back are average. However, all sizes have their uses. Whole small ones make ideal baits for eels. Big crabs can be used whole for bass and large species, cut in half or quarters for the smaller species, or for use as a tip bait.

Bait size is particularly important in relation to hook size because a large crab bait will mask a small hook and prevent it from working efficiently.

TOP TIPS

◆ Ask your tackle dealer for peelers that will be suitable for the time you are fishing. If you are going that day you want crabs about to shed their shell. If you are going at the end of the week, harder crabs will stay alive until then.

◆ Pull off the very end segment of one of the crab's legs to test if it's a peeler. A white sinew is revealed if the crab is not a peeler, while a replacement segment shows on one that is ready.

◆ You can easily test a crab to see if it is ready by pressing under the shell, behind the legs. If there is some give or a small crack starting to appear your peeler is ready.

◆ Remove all the shell and lungs from the crab if you are fishing for small fish, because these will impede the hook point. Similarly, removing the lungs when freezing down your peeler will ensure that it will stay in top condition until ready for use.

◆ Don't be tempted to use the heavy bait cotton. Modern lightweight elastic cotton is easier to remove and doesn't put the fish off. Species like eels are likely to shy away from baits that are wrapped in too much cotton. In fact, sometimes it pays not to use any cotton at all.

◆ A peeler crab must be just about to shed its shell.

BAITING UP PEELER CRABS

There are two basic ways to bait peeler and both involve removing all of the crab's shell first. The hook is then threaded through the crab's body via the leg sockets. This system is the most efficient either using a whole or half crab. Finally secure with lightweight elastic cotton.

Size 1 to 1/0 hooks are ideal for a half a peeler for flounders and most small species. Size 2 or 4 are best for eels because of their smaller mouths. A size 3/0 is about right for use with a whole peeler. You may need a size 6/0 large whole edible or velvet swimming peeler.

1 The bits and pieces that you need include bait, hook, scissors, elastic cotton.
2 First, remove all of the crab's shell.
3 Now remove the lungs.
4 Use the crab whole or cut in half.
5 Now it is ready for the hook.
6 Thread the hook through the crab's body, via the leg sockets.
7 Secure with lightweight elastic cotton.
8 Try this optional extra if you like – tip off with a leg.
9 Your crab bait is now ready to go, with another half ready to bait up.

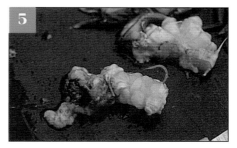

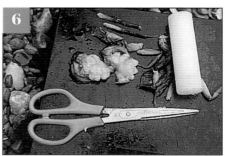

Winter worm shortages

In this question-and-answer session, we try to get to the bottom of a perennial problem

Q WHY IS THERE ALWAYS A SHORTAGE OF LUGWORM IN WINTER?

A Shortening daylight hours are mostly to blame because they so restrict digging time. Cold, wet weather also has the effect of driving the worm deeper or in the case of rain, washing the casts off the sand, which makes the densest patches difficult to locate.

Q WHY ARE LUGWORM ALWAYS SMALLER IN WINTER?

A Shortening daylight hours, neap tides and cold weather limit the time diggers can work, so in many cases they move closer to the shoreline to maximise time and the number of worm they dig. Remember they need to dig enough to make the job worthwhile, so a drop in worm size is inevitable in some places.

Q IS THERE ANY WAY THAT I CAN ENSURE A REGULAR SUPPLY OF LUGWORM?

A It's advisable to order lugworm in advance, especially in winter. Don't

◄ Black or yellowtail are tough and stay on the hook longer

travel to the coast expecting all the dealers to have plenty in stock. Phone before going to make sure of a supply.

Even then, severe weather can affect returns, so it's always advisable to take an alternative bait, such as squid or fish. The only guaranteed way to ensure a supply of lugworm is to dig your own. All anglers should have a go at this at one time or another – then they would really appreciate the fact that winter lugworm digging is not an easy matter.

◄ You will need less lugworm in winter.

► Expect a reduction in worm size in winter.

Q WHAT ARE THE ALTERNATIVE BAITS TO LUGWORM THAT REALLY WORK?

A There are a number of winter alternatives to lugworm, although the results they bring do depend upon where you are fishing. Generally you can get away with slightly inferior baits on the boat, but on the shore, bait quality and type is much more important.

Squid, ragworm, fish, mussel, frozen peeler crab and razorfish, shellfish and frozen lugworm all work, given the right conditions and places.

Q HOW MANY LUGWORM SHOULD I BUY FOR A DAY'S FISHING FROM THE SHORE OR BOAT?

A One thing is certain in the depths of winter and that is that crab, shrimp and other bait robbers are less active, so you will need less bait. Five or six score of common lugworm is plenty for the average shore session with two rods. Take along a box of squid as well if you are after cod and whiting.

Slightly more lugworm may be required from the boat. Bigger worm, such as yellowtails, are valuable, too – they nearly always bring better results.

A box of calamari squid allows you an alternative bait, as well as bulking up baits.

Q IN YOUR OPINION, WHICH ARE THE BEST LUGWORM?

A The two main species of lugworm are the large, thick-skinned black or yellowtail worm and the softer, often watery, common lugworm. Both have their particular uses and good points.

Black or yellowtails are tough and stay on the hook longer than commons. They are also far more juicy, making them ideal for cod. Common lugworm are more compact and a better size for small fish.

A number of common lugworm on the hook also means that blood and scent is released gradually. You have the advantage of several scent containers rather than when using one worm only.

Tailpiece

When the shark bites! This is what the fishing life is all about... here a dinghy angler enjoys a satisfying day of fishing for blue shark off Smerwick in south-west Ireland.